MEASURING CULTURE
A Paradigm for the Analysis of Social Organization

MEASURING CULTURE

*A Paradigm for the Analysis of Social
Organization*

by
JONATHAN L. GROSS *and* STEVE RAYNER

Introduction by MARY DOUGLAS

Columbia University Press New York 1985

Library of Congress Cataloging in Publication Data

Gross, Joanathan L.
Measuring culture.

Bibliography: p.
Includes index.
1. Culture—Mathematical models.   2. Social structure—
Mathematical models.   3. Corporate culture—Mathematical
models.   4. Risk perception—Mathematical models.
5. Culture—Data processing.   6. Social structure—Data
processing.   7. Corporate culture—Data processing.
8. Risk perception—Data processing.   I. Rayner, Steve.
II. Title.
GN506.G76 1985   306'.028'5   84-23821

ISBN 0-231-06032-7
Columbia University Press
New York   Guildford, Surrey
Copyright ©1985 Columbia University Press
All rights reserved

Printed in the United States of America

Clothbound editions of Columbia University Press books are
Smyth-sewn and printed on permanent and durable acid-free paper.

To
Rena Lea Gross
and to
Harry and Esmé Rayner

Contents

Preface

An Overview of Grid/Group Analysis

Underlying any description of a culture there is a comparison, either to one or more other explicitly identified cultures or to the totality of whatever is already familiar. Thus, even if a description completely avoids making judgments, it is necessarily comparative. This monograph is concerned with a particular way of systematizing the comparisons, called *grid/group analysis*.

Grid/group analysis is a method for comparing organizations, communities, and other social units, large and small, according to the strength of two factors in the social environment. These factors, called *grid* and *group,* can both be represented on an ordinal scale with fractional values from 0 to 1.

The critical feature of these scales is that between any two points, there is a continuum of additional possibilities. Unlike interval scales, however, there are no invariant units of grid or group. (By way of contrast, the units for any of the usual interval scales of temperature are degrees, and an increase of one degree conveys the same meaning at any temperature.) Thus, any conceivable combination of values of grid and group corresponds to a point in a one-by-one square diagram.

Grid and group are polythetic properties of the social structure. That is, to derive the numerical scores for grid and group, we must examine several different aspects of a cultural environment. The composite grid score measures the overall strength of the system of categorical distinctions, such as boss and worker, or adult, adolescent, and child. The composite group score measures the extent to which the behavior of individual members depends on their membership in a definable social unit.

While the desire to quantify the complexity and strength of social structure may seem itself to be ambitious, we want eventually to press much further. We will not be content simply to describe and measure patterns of social structure as described in this book. The overall aim of grid/group analysis is to elucidate a consistent relationship between the structure of social organizations and the patterns of ideas and behavior that they sustain.

General claims that social environment affects behavior and attitudes are unassailable. However, grid/group theory asserts a highly specific hypothesis, which leaves it accessible to challenge. This hypothesis is that different organizations with the same combinations of grid and group scores will reflect the same cultural patterns of behavior and attitudes, whether the locality is an African village, a New York corporate office, or a submarine.

Four Characteristic Patterns

The grid/group typology suggests that there are as few as four prototypical patterns of culture. Each consists of a characteristic behavioral pattern and an accompanying justificatory cosmology. Each cosmology extends, for example, to attitudes toward competition and cooperation, to concepts of good and evil in personal or community decision-making, and to the organizational structure of families, businesses, and other institutions.

To demonstrate our paradigm, we have developed in detail a single example, which is concerned with the reactions of people to high-technology risk. Specifically, we consider how representatives of each of the four prototypical cultural configurations perceive the hazards arising from the decision of a utility company to locate a nuclear power plant close to their homes.

Of the many possible contexts we might have explored to illustrate the connection between grid/group scores and behavior, risk perception seemed particularly appropriate, because its understanding is so important in the formation of public policy. We hope it is clear to our readers that we could have used this same paradigm in other settings, such as corporate mergers, schism in religious movements, or the analysis of family relationships.

We thought that risk perception would have wide appeal, since nearly everyone, in all parts of the world, frequently faces decisions involving a balancing of risks and rewards. In some urban cultures, such a decision might be where it is safe to cross the street. Others involve many more people and high economic and social stakes. A toy manufacturer runs the risk that the market for hula hoops, skateboards, or Rubik's cubes will collapse before the Christmas sales rush. Elsewhere, a farmer might need to decide whether the increased yield obtainable by harvesting a week later is worth the increased risk of storm damage. Often the risk is largely borne by persons with little or no control over the decision. For instance, a diplomat's brinkmanship might lead his countrymen into war.

Our hypothesis is that perceptions of risk by persons in the business, politics, games, and sports of modern societies are subject to cultural biases that are measurably the same as the perceptions of risk by persons in traditional societies. Modern man may be ready to recognize a link between risk perception and culture in a world where child-death or leprosy are the attendant risks of adultery, or where folk hide their bodily secretions for fear that they will fall into the hands of malevolent witches. He is often reluctant to recognize the link between his own cultural context and his perceptions of risk.

Of course, policymakers acknowledge that social or psychological conditioning as well as political or economic interests may color their fellow citizens' perceptions of risk. Nevertheless, they often express a naive conceit that the validity of a layman's perceptions of the importance of some risk compares unfavorably to an expert's value-free assessment of the probabilities and magnitudes of alternative outcomes. The issue, to some of them, of different risk perceptions is reduced to a question of greater or lesser accuracy, of how well someone is capable of envisaging what a probability of one in six, or one in three, really means.

Such a viewpoint pays insufficient heed to the problem that cultural bias is already present in the selection of the evidence on which the mathematical assessment of probability is based. Different perceivers can, and do, legitimately disagree about the figures and values used to calculate the probability of an outcome, as well as over whether any particular value for that probability is acceptable (De Finetti 1974). It is our contention that the four prototypical patterns of culture exert a strong hold over the selection of the evidence that determines a mathematical assessment of risk, just as they do over the selection of concerns within the most exotic societies. Accordingly, we have chosen a contemporary setting for our example. We imagine that our measurement method would be fundamentally the same in any other social setting.

Moreover, even if we suppose that an expert can accurately calculate the objective probabilities of each outcome, the payoff (plus or minus) of each possible outcome is intrinsically a cultural matter. To a stable neighborhood, the cultural cost of dislocation is very high, whereas to a bedroom suburb of upwardly mobile executives, the cost in cultural terms might be negligible.

Only within a cultural context can one judge whether an individual's behavior tends to optimize his expected utility because the value of each payoff is primarily a cultural matter, which, despite the efforts of cost/benefit analysts, cannot be reduced to a dollars-and-cents matter. Appraising whether it is preferable to get a job promotion or to avoid a divorce, according to rational choice models derived from economics, is an error in modeling human behavior.

The four prototype patterns of culture were first identified by Mary Douglas in *Natural Symbols* (1970), where she also formulated the concepts of grid and group. She further developed the theory in *Cultural Bias* (1978). Our present concern is making the theory operational. To this end, we have invented the EXACT model. ("EXACT" is an approximate acronym.) Empirical data are to be collected in accordance with the features of the abstract model. Then the grid and group scores are calculated in an unambiguous and reproducible way.

We make two adventurous assumptions. First, there is a strong correlation between grid/group scores and specific behavior/attitude patterns. Second, if the grid/group environment for a social unit is changed, then behavior and attitudes will catch up with the structural changes.

It is not a simple matter to test either claim, because attitudes and behavior are complicated phenomena. In this book, we treat descriptions of ideas and attitudes as relatively nonproblematic because they are commonplace state-of-the-art procedures in anthropology and psychology. Ethnographic *thick description* such as is advocated by Geertz (1973) already provides a clear paradigm for this side of the grid/group analysis. The present lack, that we seek to redress, is of a paradigm for making reproducible measurements of the behavioral patterns of the social unit that maintain the described cosmology.

The method we have developed for observing behavior is painstaking. Moreover, the identification of a behavioral pattern is not absolutely a clear-cut matter. Traits like competitiveness, egalitarianism, ritualism, and aloofness can probably be perceived to some extent in nearly all societies. Thus, we must be prepared to make judgments about matters of degree, not just about presence or absence.

We expect that it will be easier to perform a definitive test on the second claim than on the first. That is, it seems easier to substantiate a judgment that a particular organization has evolved to become, say, less competitive internally and more ritualistic, than to prove that one organization is more competitive or less ritualistic than another.

The present work does not attempt to demonstrate the empirical validity of either claim. Our example is a thought experiment and does not therefore constitute proof of these hypotheses. We do, however, aim to establish a paradigm for measuring social organization that will permit us in future to test its hypothetical match with a predicted cosmology of ideas. Since cosmology can never be measured directly, but only described, the ability to measure organizational behavior is the first step in the development of a comprehensive technique for measuring culture.

The formulation of grid/group analysis in this book is the product of a collaboration between a mathematician interested in quanitification and modeling and an anthropologist whose background is in philosophy and the methodology of social science. Our alliance has produced an explicit description of the ethonographic techniques and mathematical methods appropriate for grid/group analysis.

Some readers might be suspicious of attempts at pursuing numerical precision in a qualitative social science such as anthropology or history. Perhaps it will allay their fears to know that the authors do not seek to reduce the whole range of human experience to numbers or spots on a graph. On the contrary, we see our efforts as a humanistic enterprise, developing a comparative device for social systems. Our method is capable of illuminating and appreciating the complex connection between the formative pressures exerted by a social environment and the culture-creative responses of individuals to those pressures.

Acknowledgments

This book could not have been written but for support from the personal research funds allocated to Mary Douglas by the Russell Sage Foundation.

John Barnes, Joseph Fulda, James Hampton, Miriam Lee Kaprow, and Stephen Seidman reviewed our manuscript with critical care. In preparing the final draft, we have tried to answer as many as possible of their queries and objections. Of course, we accept the responsibility for those that remain unanswered. Douglas Clark, Nancy Groce, Hank Gross, David Ozonoff, Harry Rayner, and Michael Thompson also made helpful comments at various stages.

Karen O'Rourke typed and retyped the penultimate draft until we got it right; Madge Spitaleri deciphered some of the early handwritten versions and typed them.

The program to compute guide and group predicate scores in the appendix was prepared by Avraham Leff.

We are grateful to them all.

Introduction

MARY DOUGLAS

As an exercise in the methodology of social comparison, this volume explains itself; as a book it needs to be introduced by a sketch of the large issues which could be tested or better stated by its means. It is particularly vulnerable to misunderstanding since its place is at the point where psychology and sociology meet, one of the least well-charted areas of contemporary social thought.

I will start with a list of a few questions which are frequently posed and which in the manner of their asking reveal assumptions about the relation of individuals to their surrounding social environment. For example in industry: the declining or near stationary rates of industrial productivity in certain Western nations used to be largely explained in terms of the ratio of capital to manpower, but now there is an increasing tendency to look to the pattern of incentives affecting the labor force. The morale of the workers is as much an explicit concern in peacetime as the morale of troops in war, but morale remains a mysterious subject. Again, where attention is turned to differential rates of success in schooling, at every level there is a focus on the social conditions that mitigate or enhance innate capacity to learn. The stating of each of these much-discussed issues begs assumptions about the response of the individual to the social context, where it is supportive, liberating, or repressive. Yet the state of theory about how social resources and constraints act on the individual is impressionistic and incoherent.

There is a striking vagueness about how society works compared with the elaboration of input/output or stimulus/response theories about the individual psyche. The same lack of balance, as between social influences and individual ratiocination shows in many other matters, over the whole range of social issues. Psychopathology depends upon some clear characterization of the kinds of social support or failure of support that may account for clinical depression or mania or suicide. The vast literature on anomie and anomia has not produced an account of social influences that serves the limited scope of those problems, still less an account that would serve for disciplining and enlightening the discussion of production incentives for workers or learning in children. Yet these are not peripheral matters, but central to the concerns of a liberal democratic industrial society.

I am tempted more and more to believe that the political primacy of liberal principles has unintentionally led the compartmentalization of knowledge to this peculiar impasse. Nothing else could account for the hard clear focus on the concept of the isolated individual while the individual's social being is put in the shade. It is as if recognition of any constraints upon individual cognition which may come from social interaction would be a philosophical embarrassment. Yet, for the full understanding of individual freedom, the social context needs to be put under scrutiny and schematized.

Such a systematic, theoretical framework is not only needed for the discussion of incentives and controls on aspirations and cognition but for the discussion of social influences in history, literature, and the sociology of science. How can anyone talk about cultural differences, allocating, say, a certain intellectual bias to womankind or explaining revolutions and wars in terms of the rise or decline of religious influence, unless some fairly precise methods of assessing the relation between culture and socioeconomic pressures is at hand—and used? How can scholars seriously claim to be disentangling genetic from social influences, say in theories of criminality, educability, or selective migration, unless they use some method of assessing the social influences at a given time and place? This volume contributes such a method but the chances of it being used well depend on the state of the art in a cluster of sociological disciplines wherein a state of confusion has often been signaled, but not remedied.

One strong line of attack on a mechanistic view of the human interaction with society came to me through reading Alvin Gouldner's *The Coming Crisis of Western Sociology*.[1] This showed that in 1972, in spite of earlier distinguished criticisms, a legalistic and robotlike description of role performance is credited in sociological theory.[2] No flexible interactionist approach and no theory of culture yet addresses functional questions. These powerful broadsides might have encouraged cognitive science and psychology to recognize the gap and try to fill it with a balanced theory of social behavior. But what kind of sensitive feedback relates individuals to each other through their jointly fabricated medium of culture is still a question unposed.

Instead of grappling systematically with the social aspect of the problem, one trend has moved the other way, denying the strength of psyche's relation with society, withdrawing into phenomenology. Here one can concentrate freely on the processes of category negotiation. This is a far cry from complaining that sociologists treat culture as a solid thing, a rigid medium immersed in which individuals have no choice but to internalize its structure and respond to its cues. The pendulum has swung to the other extreme. Everyone now knows that cultural categories can be renegotiated and that everyone is actively engaged in doing so. Then culture comes to be treated as utterly pliable, even transparent: the only barriers to renegotiation lie in the distribution of power, so now culture can be treated as a mere veil over transactions, to be discounted. Thus, theory is set back to examining the conditions of *force majeure* governing the exchange between individuals.[3] The real logjam is unmoved: culture does not enter as an explanation of behavior. There is still the block to understanding how the universe of humanly fabricated categories that emerges from transactions acts sometimes as a lag on the perception of what is possible and sometimes as a spur to individual creativity.

In his presidential address to the American Psychological Association in 1975, Don Campbell repeatedly emphasized the need for a theory of culture that would explain the stabilizing processes in society.[4] How can individuals be restrained from wrecking the larger community by their self-interested behavior, and how can a theory which starts from the individual's pursuit of self-interest ever account for such social solidarity as there may be?

A recent review by Kenneth and Mary Gergen shows how weakly the data of social psychology are secured.[5] The Gergens have a neat classification of theories in the sociobehavioral sciences. They distinguish them on two dimensions. One scale shows how much the locus of explanation is found in the person or in the situation; theories of the latter kind tend to treat the individual as a passive respondent to situational pressures; theories of the former type are more voluntaristic, more concerned to acknowledge individual freedom of choice. On another scale, they rank theories according to the strength of the pressures the theory assumes to be acting upon the individual, a control dimension. When they have distinguished weak and strong control, internal and external locus of explanation, they allocate radical behaviorism and dialectial materialism to slots with strong control by mechanisms external to the individual, and psychoanalysis, Piagetian theory, cognitive and trait theory as examples of strong control attributed to mechanisms internal to the individual. Phenomenology and hermeneutics are examples of theories which take the person as the locus of explanation and expect control to be weak.

The Gergens use this framework to trace a revolutionary shift of focus within the sociobehavioral sciences, from strong to weak control and from external to internal mechanisms. But they can find no professional, theoretical reason for this change of theory and no empirical grounds either. No sure distinction can even be made between the states counted as internal to the psyche and those counted as external. The internal states are postulated from externally visible behavior and vice versa, the external events are only described through categories which restate the presumed psychic processes.

For example, an assessment of the external world enters the psychologist's theory in the forms of complaints of persecution, but are the persecuting features of the outside world really present or mere projections of the subject's inner world? The data being hopelessly confounded, no reasons based on the state of the art explain the theoretical shift. The Gergens conclude that the validation of one theoretical bias against another has little to do with the theorizing itself, but rather comes from an area of meta-theory validated by preferences in the society at large and adopted (who can say how consciously?) by the psychologists. This subtle and sophisticated review could be destructive for further work in these disciplines. Almost cynically, the Gergens suggest that since validation does not come from autonomous intellectual disciplines, in psychology the best recourse is for theory to go along with the meta-theoretical mood of the outside world.

However, this radical criticism goes too far. If it were true that the independent identity of elements of the theories had to be assured empirically before the theories are allowed to get off the ground, even the hard sciences would have a bad time. The more fundamental weakness of psychology is not in the labile nature of the facts upon which theories are constructed, but in the partial, sketchy, and haphazard nature of the theorizing. In a young science, where consensus is missing, questions of identity plague discussion, but as theory develops, many of these questions dissolve in the coherent account of interactions and transformations by which a theory gains control over a larger and more complexly differentiated field.[6] The quandary of the behavioral sciences, so devastatingly analyzed by Kenneth and Mary Gergen, could be resolved by developing a functional theory of culture to organize the scene that at present shifts so disconcertingly from inside to outside of the psyche. An approach to cultural analysis that stays explicitly on the outside and develops a few theories about how culture and society are organized together could be a start.

Grid/group analysis is part of an approach whose data are either actions or statements in defense of actions. It looks at public allegiances, tributes, incorporations, and rejections, seeking positivistically to construct from unquestionable bases a social environment that people say constrains them, or act as if it constrains them. The approach ventures to say nothing about the psyche, only that in creating a form of society, people publicly espouse beliefs and values which are its cultural counterpart. Then arises the question of how to assess the visible social part of the social framework. This is where grid/group analysis is expected to help.

This volume does not promise in any way to establish order in the theoretical disarray. Its objective is more modest. It provides a handbook for anyone desirous of checking out the pressures of constraint and opportunity which are presumed to shape individual response to the social environment. The pressures proposed are selected with a view to testing a theory which runs against the tide. By far the largest analytical interest in the concept of culture comes from anthropology. Apart from some notable exceptions, the important work has been American and has emphasized cultural evolution and processes of cultural change.[7] But how can change be understood without some parallel work on stable structures? Without typology, the process of change cannot be tracked.

A different route of approach to culture which will be aided by the methods described here focuses on mutually stabilizing the processes as between an actual physical manifestation of power and authority on the one hand and on the other, the categories of thought which are used to promote its stability or to undo it. Certain patterns of value and certain beliefs have always been associated in Western thought with certain social structures. The theory assumes that these associations are not random and can be schematized. Is it true that bureaucracy encourages traditionalism and legalism? Is it true that market conditions breed attitudes supportive of free enterprise? This analysis would put the relation differently. How long could bureaucracy last if it did not engender commitment to tradition and the primacy of the whole over the part? Presumably, if it fails to engender the appropriate commitments those individuals who are doing poorly in the prevailing distributive system will seek to overturn it. Consequently, the central issue is not cultural change. The amazing thing that needs to be investigated is cultural stability, whenever and wherever it is found.

So this method of grid/group analysis is a tool for testing. It does not help the researcher to know what are the values and ideas that constitute the local culture, but it does help to be able to locate them in the appropriate part of the population. The ideas to which people consent have to be identified by other means. This methodological tool makes more precise the nature of the individual's response to society by staying at the level of social relations. It never tries to dive into the murky area of what is happening inside the psyche. It is devised for a theory that merely expects differences of opinion to be found in differently constructed social universes. The method of Gross and Rayner shows how the social locations of differing opinions can be mapped, and that is quite a start.

What Gross and Rayner have christened the EXACT model has strong theoretical implications written into it. The underlying assumption is that a social unit of a particular pattern endures by the supporting commitments of its population and that this commitment will be manifest in the admonitions, excuses, and moral judgments by which the people mutually coerce one another into conformity. These public statements are the verbal counterpart of actions which draw the material shape of the institutions in space. If they salute hierarchy as an ordering principle, their acts of deference will be visible. If they say they are committed to individual enterprise, they can be seen making loans or preventing restrictive practices. If they say they are committed to equality, they can be seen forcing leveling procedures upon one another. If they say they are committed to life within a group, it will show in the way they spend their time together.

The difference between what people say and what they do is not necessarily important. Obviously, not all words are required all the time to lend their support to action. But there will be moments of truth: when a misfortune strikes,[8] the acceptable explanations will need to be plausible to people who have constructed their universe in a certain way. Or when a crisis comes, alignments that were loose and ambiguous will be tightened, and statements of value will be clarified. This form of cultural analysis focuses on the testing times when people stand up and are counted and what they say then. It looks specially for the values that would need to be publicly supported if the institutional forms are to survive, or if there is some pressure to make words match deeds. Arthur Stinchcombe has recently pointed to the importance of uncovering the moral structure that underlies institutional life;[9] this exercise seeks to uncover the institutional structures that uphold the moral life.

The EXACT model is well designed for this purpose. It is not easy to decide whether a community at one time is more committed to group solidarity than it was at some earlier time. That happens to be a favorite judgment bandied back and forth among American historians without agreed methods for settling the issue. Gross and Rayner have thought of five indices of a strong group: proportion of time spent in the group compared with total allocatable time; frequency of meeting; closeness of interlocking character links; the proportion of shared to unshared links and strength of the boundary of the group. Two communities may turn out on the basis of such comparisons to be very strong in group solidarity, but the quality of social life in the group can be quite different. The checking and testing of these indices of group can show whether the apparent solidarity depends entirely on shared economic conditions, or whether the solidary community is riven with strong factions.

Grid measures quite a distinct set of indices which tell even more about the feel of living in a community. It will be different if its members try to make its style egalitarian or if they have organized a clear pecking order. Furthermore, it will face different organizational problems according to these differences. An orderly hierarchy with a clear division of roles is well adapted to getting work done, but it will have underdogs and topdogs and so will need theories of social justice to explain to those underneath why they should accept the present distribution. Crises occur all the time and at crises these theories will be evoked and the attentive investigator will hear words that justify the behavior that is seen. The same goes for the other institutional types. Consequently, the special interest of EXACT is the ingenuity expended on developing the other dimension to set against group. This grid dimension is intended to capture and assess all the other kinds of constraints which members of society bear and which are not necessarily by definition constraints of belonging to a group. Between the two axes of grid and group, a great range of variation in the quality of social life can be charted. Cultural analysis expects the values involved to differ accordingly.

In working on this approach, I have provisionally suggested kinds of moral values and theories of the world that would seem *prima facie* good candidates for demonstrating the institutional support that is sought in cosmological ideas. Sometimes the examples have been offered for illustrative purposes as most of those cited in *Cultural Bias*. Some have received a preliminary working out as part of an analysis. For example, in *Risk and Culture* the structure of groups involved in the environmental movement was compared with their stated aims in order to demonstrate the predicted compatibilities. The objective is a general theory of how packaged bundles of cosmological ideas are assorted to the institutional structures which they stabilize. As I see it, all the work lies ahead, in the testing of links and refining of concepts which EXACT promises to make possible, and which will be a very long task. Meanwhile some interesting suggestions along these lines have appeared and illustrate the diversity of questions about culture, psyche, and society that can be investigated by this method. The history of electromagnetism, preference among forms of business accounting, and patterns of workplace crime afford unexpected and welcome application of the basic idea.[10]

Naturally, the EXACT model is entirely abstract. It presents a method for stating a problem about social variation as a set of interacting ratios. Anyone who plans to use EXACT will be forced to think hard about the society being examined; very likely some of the suggested grid criteria will be abandoned if they do not apply to the case in hand. Others will be refined, multiplied, or new ones invented to get a closer understanding of critical social interactions. The five grid criteria chosen here rely strongly upon those used for assessing the group. For example, the group clues tell us about the frequency and closeness of interactions, but it makes a great difference if these are asymmetrical, carrying clearly defined penalties or rewards. The group in which everyone can take up any role is quite different from that which defines specialized parts for its members to play. EXACT separates neatly the kinds of communications which go on and then allows them to be rejoined in the composite picture.

In using EXACT the investigator will need to use ethnographic judgment just as much as in any research design. It would be absurd to expect the same indices to apply to any question whatever. If it is the solidarity of Sunday School teachers with the parents of their pupils, one set of clues will be appropriate; if it is the solidarity of the work force with its union, another—of course. The investigator uses EXACT as a framework upon which to draw the delicate threads of a net that will capture the information that is relevant, sort it out, and use it for constructing a basis for cultural comparison.

The first step is to choose a problem for which the method is adapted. The next step needs two aspects of behavior to be coordinated. One is the description of cultural categories as they are being used. The other, outlined in this book, is the description of the population using them. When they are brought together, the resulting cultural analysis should go far to explain bias in attitudes and values as well as in theoretical preferences.

Notes

1. Alvin W. Gouldner, *The Coming Crisis of Western Sociology* (London: Heineman, 1970).

2. Herbert A. Simon and James S. March, *Organizations* (New York: Wiley, 1958).

3. F. G. Bailey, *Stratagems and Spoils* (Oxford: Blackwell, 1969). Peter Blau, *Exchange and Power in Social Life* (New York: Wiley, 1964). Abner Cohen, *Two Dimensional Man: An Essay on the Anthropology of Power and Symbolism in Complex Society* (Berkeley: University of California Press, 1974).

4. Donald T. Campbell, "On the Conflicts Between Biological and Social Evolution and Between Psychology and Moral Tradition," *American Psychologist* (December 1975), 30 (12):1103–1126.

5. Kenneth J. Gergen and Mary M. Gergen, "Form and Function in the Explanation of Human Conduct" in P. Secord, ed., *Paradigms in the Social Sciences* (Beverly Hills: Sage, 1982.)

6. W. V. O. Quine, "Natural Kinds," in *Essays in Ontological Relativity* (New York: Columbia University Press, 1969).

7. Richard D. Alexander, "Evolution and Culture," in N. A. Chagnon and W. Irons, eds, *Evolutionary Biology and Human Social Behavior: An Anthropological Perspective* (Boston: PWS, 1979)

8. This draws upon E. E. Evans-Pritchard, *Nuer Religion* (Oxford: Clarendon Press, 1956) and refers to a more extended principle of accountability based upon it. See Mary Douglas, *Evans-Pritchard* (New York: Penguin, 1980).

9. Arthur L. Stinchcombe, "The Deep Structure of Moral Categories: Eighteenth-Century French Stratification and the Revolution," in Ino Rossi, ed., *Structural Sociology* (New York: Columbia University Press, 1982), pp. 66–95.

10. Mary Douglas, *Cultural Bias* (Royal Anthropological Institute Occasional Paper No. 35, 1978. Republished in *In The Active Voice* (London: Routledge and Kegan Paul, 1982); Mary Douglas and Aaron Wildavsky, *Risk and Culture: An Essay on the Selection of Technological and Environmental Dangers* (Berk: California University Press, 1982); Kenneth L. Caneva, "What Should We Do with the Monster? Electromagnetism and the Psychosociology of Knowledge," in E. Mendelsohn and Y. Elkana, eds., *Sciences and Cultures: Sociology of the Sciences,* (D. Reidel, 1981), 5:101–131; Kenneth P. Gee, "Financial Control," Inaugural Lecture delivered on November 19, 1980, University of Salford; Gerald Mars, *Cheats at Work: An Anthropology of Workplace Crime,* (London: Allen and Unwin, 1982).

MEASURING CULTURE
A Paradigm for the Analysis of Social Organization

CHAPTER ONE

A BACKGROUND TO GRID/GROUP ANALYSIS

It is somewhat fashionable to dismiss culture as a mere epiphenomenon of economic and political organization. Culture has seldom been invested with a great deal of explanatory power, except among the quaint tribe of anthropologists. Moreover, even anthropologists have commonly presented culture as the sum of customs, usages, traditions, myths, and rituals to be found among a discrete people, tribe class, or nation. So why do we bother with cultural explanations?

The reason is that in recent years a transformation has occurred. Modern anthropology is largely concerned with the dynamic interaction of a number of cultures that share the same location in time and space. There are stark contrasts, such as agrarian and rural communities within developing societies, bourgeois and proletarian life-styles coexisting in industrial nations, and black and white social networks juxtaposed in neighborhoods of modern cities.

1.1 An Updated View of Culture

In a dynamic setting, culture is much more than an artifact produced by a given set of people: it is the common way that a community of persons makes sense of the world. Indeed, this shared interpretive framework is precisely what defines a culture, whether the members are black intellectuals, white laborers, or bushman hunters. Under this interpretation, moreover, the sharing of culture has been increasingly accepted as the defining criterion for the specific units of anthropological analysis, rather than as a set of characteristics exhibited by geographically defined societies.

Understanding the culture of a social unit tells us how its members define themselves in relation to members of other communities and how they define their standing among themselves. Hence, the emerging concept of culture, as the way in which people make sense of their world, may explain why people do what they do, as well as why they do it in one way and not another.

In this book we illustrate our new method of analysis by an example in which different social groupings among the inhabitants of a fictitious New England town engage in a controversy over the location of a nuclear reactor. Of course, it is widely held, with good reason, that nuclear power might present grave risks to the surrounding population. Economic rationalists argue that individuals decide to take a risk by first weighing its potential costs and benefits and then opting for the course of action that they think will maximize the advantages that will accrue. This assumption of rational decisions, popular among professional policymakers, is called the *utility principle*.

A widely recognized problem with the utility principle, particularly at the formalized level of cost-benefit analysis, is its awkwardness in explaining a choice between qualitatively different costs and benefits. For one example, how can the aesthetic, historical, and spiritual costs of demolishing an ancient church to build a new airport be weighed against the economic benefits which that airport might bring, not only to the locality that loses its traditional place of worship, but to an entire region or even a whole country? (Self 1975). For another, how can the statistical certainty of loss of life through an industrial process be balanced against the loss of employment which outlawing the process might bring? These are not just hypothetical questions, but ones that have been the focus of major public policy debates in Britain and the United States during the last ten years. Many ingenious attempts have been made to rescue balancing radically different utilities (Schwing and Albers 1980) but none has succeeded in

reconciling disagreements about values in the world of real policy-
making.

When people choose an uneconomic path by avoiding risk—or
in some cases at the opposite extreme by reckless pursuit of it—
the pure economic rationalists can fall back on only one explanation: to wit, those concerned have failed, through ignorance,
false consciousness, quirkiness, or even willful malice, to make
a correct assessment of the costs and benefits. By way of contrast, our view of culture offers a much richer range of explanation of why people choose options that some experts deem
outside their best interests. It is increasingly recognized that the
maximization of anticipated utilities is only a second step. It must
be preceded by the ranking of diverse utilities which, in our view,
is primarily a phenomenon of culture, not of economics.

Cultural studies tell us that attitudes towards risk, and towards
everything else, vary according to the way people make sense of
their experiences (Thompson 1980 a & b; 1982 a & b; Douglas
and Wildavsky 1982). In particular, the quality of riskiness is
ascribed to different actions from one culture to the next, according to the different cosmological frameworks in which the persons in different cultures interpret the events in their lives.

Our perspective that shared culture defines the social unit leads
to an examination of culture as a general regulatory mechanism
for human behavior. Culture is a set of plans, instructions, and
rules, or, less purposively, a means of social accounting. This
concept of culture as a control system starts from the assumption
that much of human thought is basically both social and public.
As Ryle (1949) has suggested, thinking does not take place in
the head, but all around us. What we think with is not a private
metaphysical mind, but with words, pictures, gestures, actions,
and both natural and manufactured objects. Indeed, we assign
symbolic meaning so as to impose some sort of order and coher-
ence on the stream of events. In so doing, we sift and filter our
sensations of the world.

In the process of making the whole business comprehensible,
some perceptions are admitted, some rejected, and others combined or broken down. If we did not filter experiences in this way

or make use of public symbols for organizing perceptions and communicating them to others, then we would be likely overwhelmed by the variety of possible interpretations that could be assigned to events. We would have to abandon intellect and discourse and thereby be forced, like the lower animals, to rely on instinct. Mankind would be reduced, as Geertz (1973) has observed, to mental basket cases.

The filtering of sensory input and the use of symbols in thought are public processes, aspects of the cultural control mechanisms. Individual decisions are made according to a shared structuring of consciousness that is readily observable. It can be seen in the organization of markets, the layout of houses, the adoption of dress codes, and indeed everywhere in the realm of public behavior.

From this standpoint, the cultural interpretation of the acceptability of risks revolves around different perceptions of what a risk is, rather than on the dichotomy of right or wrong perceptions of costs and benefits. This applies not only to the major contingencies of public policy debates, but also to more mundane choices such as where to cross the street. And, of course, such an interpretation goes beyond perceptions of risks to all aspects of everyday life.

There is a major objection to cultural relativism, a form of which is what we are proposing. This objection states that if we cannot say that there are right or wrong perceptions of the world, but only different perceptions, then public debate and political discussions would be purely concerned with matters of individual taste. It would follow, the objection continues, that criticism of other viewpoints besides one's own should be abandoned in favor of merely appreciating another person's cultural bias. Even systematic appreciation would be rendered impossible, because the range of possible cultures is infinite, and there would be presumably nothing to prevent us from choosing any one of the range more or less on whim.

If the last claim were accurate, then the objectors to cultural relativism would carry the day. Its error is that there is no reason to imagine the existence of an infinite array of incomparable cul-

tural possibilities. On the contrary, we have designed a mathematical model such that all of the various ways a social unit can
be organized are representable by only two variables. In this
book we show how these variables can be measured and applied
to the systematic analyses of cultures.

1.2 The Concepts of Group and Grid

Grid/group theory was introduced by Mary Douglas in *Natural
Symbols* and expanded in *Cultural Bias*. Fundamental cultural
constraints are organized into two polythetic variables called grid
and group. By representing these variables diagramatically on
the x- and y-axis in a plane, we can study the simultaneous effect
of both kinds of constraints.

Group

Group, the *horizontal* coordinate, represents the extent to
which people are restricted in thought and action by their commitment to a social unit larger than the individual. High group
strength results when people devote a lot of their available time
to interacting with other members of their unit. In general, the
more things they do together, and the longer they spend doing
them, the higher the group strength.

Where admission to the social unit is hard to obtain, making
the unit more exclusive and conscious of its boundary, the group
strength also tends to be high. An extreme case of high group
strength is the monastic or communal setting where private property is renounced upon entering, and the members depend on the
corporate body for all of their material and social life support.
High group strength of this sort requires a long-term commitment
and a tight identification of members with one another as a corporate entity. Individuals are expected to act on behalf of the
collective whole, and the corporate body is expected to act in the
normative interests of its members.

Group strength is low when people negotiate their way through life on their own behalf as individuals, neither constrained by, nor reliant upon, a single group of others. Instead, low-group people interact as individuals with other individuals, picking and choosing with whom they will associate, as their present preoccupations and perceived interests demand. The low-group experience is a competitive, entrepreneurial way of life where the individual is not strongly constrained by duty to other persons.

Attractive though this freedom from constraint might first appear to some of us, there is a serious disadvantage: the low-group individualist is unable to fall back on the support of his fellows should his personal fortune wane. In the high-group context, the safety net of social support is compensation for the loss of personal autonomy. Grid/group analysis ascribes to every social environment both advantages and drawbacks with respect to other possible environments.

Grid

Grid, the *vertical* coordinate, is the complementary bundle of constraints on social interaction, a composite index of the extent to which people's behavior is constrained by role differentiation, whether within or without membership of a group. Grid is high strength whenever roles are distributed on the basis of explicit public social classifications, such as sex, color, position in a hierarchy, holding a bureaucratic office, descent in a senior clan or lineage, or point of progression through an age-grade system. It is low strength when classificatory distinctions only weakly limit the range of social choices or activities open to people.

A low-grid social environment is one in which access to roles depends upon personal abilities to compete or negotiate for them, or even of formal regulations for taking equal turns. In either case, where access to roles is not dependent on any ascribed characteristics of rank or birth, we would recognize a low-grid condition. To invoke an established anthropological usage, we would say that where roles are primarily *ascribed* grid constraints are high. Where roles are primarily *achieved* grid constraints are low.

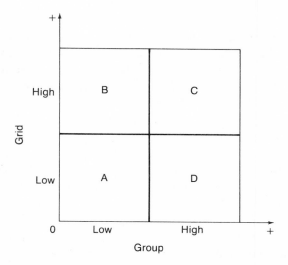

Figure 1.1. Four prototype grid/group combinations.

1.3 Prototype Grid/Group Combinations

The simultaneous consideration of high or low strength in these two dimensions of control over the individual, group commitment and grid controls, gives rise to four prototype possibilities of social life, represented in figure 1.1.

Low Grid/Low Group

Quadrant A (low grid/low group) allows the maximum options for negotiating contracts or choosing allies. Consequently, it also allows for individual mobility up and down the scale of prestige and influence. In this environment, a frontiersman or a capitalist entrepreneur might thrive, in large scale, like the American robber barons or in small scale like Brecht's *Mother Courage*. No one cares about the past or about anyone's ancestry. Each person is responsible for himself and for whomsoever else he chooses, not for the weak or the needy, unless he wills it so. There are few limitations on the pressure he may exert on others. For instance, an individual may pick up and move at any time. He may employ children to work in his factory 18 hours a day, 7 days a week. After all, he reasons, children have the freedom to do something else if they don't like the contractual terms! Personal strength and good fortune are considered a fitting basis for personal prosperity.

Examples of low-grid/low-group social organizations abound also in pre-capitalist societies. Within the Hindu caste system (Marriott 1976), the Ksatriyas, mainly warring princes and major landowners, seem to stand in quadrant A relative to the other Varna caste groups. The self-aggrandizing Kwakiutl (Benedict 1934) conform to our idea of life in this sort of environment, as do the entrepeneurial big-men who control public life in highland New Guinea (Strathern 1971). Similar behavioral patterns can be identified in ancient society, as McLeod's (1982) description of the peripatetic generals of Warring States China tells us.

High Grid/Low Group

Quadrant B (high grid/low group) is an environment in which the way persons may behave is strongly regulated according to their socially assigned classifications. It is often a hierarchical environment in which most persons are classified out of the decision-making process. Perhaps the classifying criterion is ancestry, and all roles are based on its correlatives. Or maybe the criterion is age, so that each person passes through a stream of age-related categories. Unlike quadrant A, the control exerted in this environment is not that of one person forcing his will upon another, but rather that of a whole society ready to negotiate only those deals that reinforce the pervasive social classifications.

In this environment, persons in favorable categories are protected by their classifications from many of the effects of misfortune. Moreover, along with members of unfavorable categories they will find their social options and access to resources curtailed by powerful others operating from one of the other grid/group quadrants.

Sometimes, these others will exert their control paternalistically in what they claim to be the interests of quadrant B persons. For example, social workers in Britain are able to exert a high degree of control over their clients' spending patterns through their ability to make deductions for fuel and rent payments from welfare checks at source. In contrast, it is common that the motives of those exerting control over high-grid/low-group individuals are not benign at all. The exploitation, by some industries, of outworkers, often single mothers working from home so that they can look after small children, is one such case.

Various occupations will place the constraints of a high-grid/ low-group life-style on people including door-to-door salesmen and supermarket cashiers (Mars 1982). The housebound disabled and elderly are other examples where strong social classifications and isolation create dependency on others. The stigmatization and exclusion of Spanish urban gypsies from both the benefits and responsibilities of belonging to the wider society (Kaprow 1978) would merit their inclusion in this list, alongside the Sudra caste at the bottom rung of the Varna ladder (Marriott 1976), or the rubbish-men who have failed to make the grade in Papua New Guinea (Strathern 1971). Favorable categories are harder to find here than unfavorable ones. The medieval dowager installed in a dower house by her son upon his succession to his fathers' lands and titles might be one such case.

High Grid/High Group

Quadrant C (high grid/high group) is where one might find tradition-bound institutions in which everyone knows his place, but in which that place might vary with time. Extensive security is obtained at the expense of most possibilities for overt competition and social mobility. Examples of this type of social organization include bureaucracies that base their roles on seniority (an ascribed basis) rather than merit (an achieved basis), or a cohesive tribal society with hereditary roles. Such a bureaucratic environment might occur in civil service, an educational system, a strongly unionized industry, or a peacetime military, where promotion is based on length of service rather than competitively upon relative ability. Other kinds of society that would fit this description would include the Polynesian chieftanships described by Sahlins (1963), the Hindu Brahmins (Marriott 1976), and the Chan Kingdom of ancient China (McLeod 1982).

In this environment, both prosperity and security are collective concerns. Judgment and luck tend to be collective matters in quadrant C, unlike quadrant B, where prescribed individual choices and opportunities are reserved for persons according to their categories in the system. An individual in quadrant C who goes along with the system may expect eventual rewards, unless collective misfortune intervenes. In bad times, everyone sinks together. The king might be the first to die in battle, and the captain will go down with his ship. This is very much unlike low-grid/low-group quadrant A, in which a king (who is likely to have been a usurper) might have a refuge for himself and his family prepared in advance, and in which a captain would sail off with provisions in the best lifeboat. In quadrant A, some individuals might be privately negotiating with the enemy and others too busy fighting each other for power to notice the collective threat.

Low Grid/High Group

Finally, quadrant D (low grid/high group) is a social context in which the external group boundary is typically the dominant consideration. All other aspects of interpersonal relationships are ambiguous and open to negotiation. Leadership tends to be charismatic and lacking clear rules for succession. Extreme cases are represented by certain religious and political cults whose members interact with each other on an egalitarian basis (Rayner 1979, 1982).

The suspicion of infiltration by outsiders or betrayal by group members that is rampant here is personified in Benedict's (1934) description of the Dobuans' characteristic paranoia. A more moderate case of low grid/high group is the Vaisya caste of skilled artisans who avoid inter-caste obligations that would hinder their low-grid mobility as contractual workers or traders, while they depend on high-group relations within their caste for their livelihood (Marriott 1976).

It has been observed (Ostrander 1982) that each of the four prototypes of social organization described here corresponds to certain established models in sociology and political science, especially those of Morton Fried (1967), Guy Swanson (1969), and Basil Bernstein (1971). The grid/group scheme differs from these previous models of social organization in two respects.

First, its categories are intended to be more general in application than those specifically employed to describe formal political processes or educational systems. We intend our categories to be applicable to social organization at many levels between the concept of individual socialization described by Bernstein and those of large-scale political evolution postulated by Fried. Second, the grid/group framework is especially suited to diachronic analysis of social systems undergoing change as well as synchronic comparisons of different systems.

Grid/Group as a Model of Social Change

Diachronic grid/group analysis can describe a diversity of cultural processes found in different parts of the world. The advantage in translating these processes into a grid/group framework is that it concentrates our understanding of underlying patterns of social change, in general terms applicable to all human societies, and not just on the specifics of each case.

By way of illustration, grid/group analysis can be applied to the continuous cycles of transformation between an egalitarian *gumlao* political order and a hierarchical *gumsa* system among the Kachin people of Highland Burma, described by Leach (1954) and Friedman (1975).

The Kachin are swidden agriculturalists who live in small hamlets forming a village cluster. In the egalitarian *gumlao* stage, these villages are the largest political units. The Kachin engage in community feasting, the dual purpose of which is to distribute agricultural surplus (giving prestige to the donors) and to propitiate the spirits (in order to increase the wealth of the entire community). Among *gumlao* Kachin, all community ritual is held at the village altar, giving everyone access to the local spirits. In this system, marriages are arranged between equal wife-giving and wife-taking lineages. This is a weak-grid/weak-group state relative to the *gumsa* system that grows out of it.

The *gumlao* system is supplanted by the hierarchical *gumsa* system in the following manner. By producing a greater surplus than his peers, a lineage head whose efforts or good fortune lead to good harvests increases his status by giving great feasts. His wealth also enables him to acquire more wives, and therefore children, to increase his workforce and thus expand his surpluses. His new status is further heightened through the Kachin belief that wealth is not the product of human labor, but the work of the gods. Thus, the successful lineage head is tempted to claim that his is the same lineage as that of the local spirits responsible for his success. The altars of these spirits are appropriated by this lineage chief, and moved to his house as places of family worship. Thus he establishes an hereditary basis for his preeminence.

As the brideprice of the daughters of the preeminent lineage rises, the egalitarian marriage patterns of the *gumlao* system give way to alliances governed by a political and economic hierarchy of lineages. Chiefly status of the head of the preeminent lineage may be further enhanced by territorial expansion to produce absolute surplus with the labor of debt slaves. Over several generations, particularly successful lineages acquire control over a number of villages whose own heads owe allegiance to its hereditary paramount chief, who is at the pinnacle of what has become a hierarchical *gumsa* system at high grid/high group.

But, prolonged intensive agricultural production places a heavy burden on the land. Hence it is not long before the productive forces that underlie the position of the paramount chief go into decline. The biggest weakness in the *gumsa* system seems to be inflation in the prestige goods that are used to make bridewealth payments. Inability to pay bridewealth reduces lesser aristocratic lineages to commoner status, while commoners are forced into debt-slavery. In this situation, local village leaders will rebel against their paramount chiefs, repudiate their debts, and reassert equality of lineage rank among all Kachin. Since the position of the dominant lineage in *gumsa* depends on prestige and not on power, it is unable to resist a consensual shift back to *gumlao*.

However, the underlying agricultural, economic, kinship, and religious mechanisms remain intact so that future development of surpluses is possible, and the cycle can begin again. In fact, according to Friedman, the redispersal of population in the *gumlao* stage permits the regrowth of primary forest, without which the high productivity necessary for the subsequent gumsa development would be impossible. This cycle, illustrated in figure 1.2

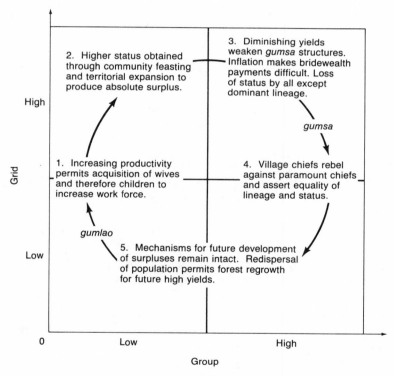

Figure 1.2. Grid/group representation of Kachin *gumlao/gumsa* cycle

takes several generations, thus allowing time for the institution-alization of lineage hierarchies, which differentiate *gumsa,* as a high-grid system, from the straightforward development of personal monopolies within a weak-grid system, such as the competition between big-men in Papua New Guinea (Strathern 1971).

The two-dimensional diagram thus presents a set of limits within which the individual can move around, or within which a social organization may develop and change. Between the lowest and the highest conceivable group strengths, there is a continuum of possibilities for grid strength. The diagram is useful both for indicating the combination of grid and group at a fixed time, and for charting social change over a period of time.

No location in the diagram could ever appear entirely favorable, except possibly from its own perspective. Even then, the phenomenon of continual change suggests that the members of most organizations are never fully satisfied.

1.4 The Concepts of Social Order and Cosmology

The objective of considering grid and group simultaneously is not merely to describe patterns of solidarity rules and social classifications governing the allocation of roles. The fundamental purpose of grid/group analysis is to provide a framework within which a cultural analyst may consistently relate differences in organizational structures to the strength of the values that sustain them.

Grid-group analysis treats ideas and values as both reflecting and constituting the experience both of belonging to a social organization and of social differentiation within the organization. In this it follows the Weberian notion that individuals negotiating their way through the organizational constraints of actively interpreting, challenging, accepting and recreating their social environment are limited to a range of arguments consistent with the constitutive premises of that environment.

At low grid, where there is little classificatory distinction between individuals and roles are not ascribed but achieved, there is the advantage that it makes no sense to argue that a person should be denied a job "because she is black" or "because it's not women's work." On the other hand, at high grid there is less ambiguity about roles and status. A benefit of a strongly regulated society is that people know how they are expected to behave at work, at home, in church, in the street, and when introduced to strangers.

The degree of collectivity experienced by people also constrains the legitimacy of the values to which they may resort to justify their actions. Where the collective pressures are weak, at low group, one would logically expect individualistic values of originality and self-reliance, in contrast with the collectivist ideology of mutual aid and responsibility which legitimates a high group social experience. One expects, therefore, that the premises involved in defining grid/group constraints within a social unit will place different pressures on the structure of beliefs that can be used to evaluate and legitimate actions taken within it. We use the term *cosmology* to describe this framework of ultimate justifications that are invoked to support the social order.

We do not expect everybody who shares a particular combination of grid and group strengths to maintain all of the cosmological attributes of their quadrant with equal conviction. We assert only that there will be a predominant collective disposition towards a particular pattern of ideas which is compatible with their experience of social organization. Of course, there will be disagreements. Neither the individual's nor the collective cosmology is fixed forever. Some persons will seek to change only their own patterns of social organization and some will seek to change their friends' and neighbors' at the same time. However, others will resist changing, both for themselves and for others.

If people wish for continuity, they will call upon familiar principles to uphold the status quo. If they wish to promote social change, then they will adopt different justifications. If the social structure changes, people will modify their cosmology to accommodate the change. If they do not, then they may find themselves classified out of society's mainstream, excluded by their fellows, or forced into defensive sectarian postures with others who are unable or unwilling to adapt.

1.5 **Why Make Grid/Group Analysis Operational?**

Douglas' presentation of grid/group analysis (1970, 1978) is a *tour de force* in which the theory is illustrated from a wide range of ethnographic and literary sources. How on earth can this theoretical model be made operational?

One wants to know exactly what kinds of observable social behavior indicate either grid or group constraints, and how grid and group constraints can be definitively distinguished. This is especially important where there are classificatory criteria for membership of social units such as men's or women's sports teams. Perhaps the toughest, and certainly the most important of all of these questions is, how can group and grid be reliably measured in such a way that valid comparisons may be made between different social organizations?

It is our intention to describe how we have made grid/group theory into a quantitative analytic technique for comparing cultural systems. We are concerned both with concrete observable social relations, the social environment that corresponds to what Radcliffe-Brown (1952) called *social structure,* and with the symbols, ideas, excuses, and justifications for actions with which people think about those relations. One might still ask what point there is to such comparisons between the cultures of different kinds of social organization. In the past, such projects were undertaken to illustrate grand theories of human development such as evolution from *status* to *contract* (Maine 1861), or from *mechanical* to *organic* solidarity (Durkheim 1893). Now that such theories are largely discredited, what need have we of the comparative project which was once the pulse of social anthropology?

First, comparison is a necessary step toward generalization. Failure to ensure that the terms of a comparison are valid invites the notorious practice of *Bongo Bongoism,* in which one pulls a generalization from under the feet of a colleague by citing the putative ethnography of other people elsewhere who appear to do something different. If a generalization is based on a comparative typology, then it is incumbent on the challenger to show that the social units under consideration are comparable with respect to the other factors on which the typology is based. Only then can the challenger claim to have found an exception that disproves the rule.

Second, social scientists want more than to make syncretic comparisons of different societies. Postwar controversies over the phenomenon of *modernization* (Bell 1973, 1980) have made the importance of social change irresistible even to the most dyed-in-the-wool functionalists. Alas, traditional social typologies have been static, with fixed hierarchies of generalizations and hard and fast dividing lines between categories—what Engels (1886) criticized as the "metaphysical mode of thought." This has brought the whole enterprise of social typology into disrepute.

So far, typologies have not been constructed in such a way as to show social change as it occurs, except through the *ad hoc* imposition of transitional subcategories. These tend to violate Ockham's razor, rather like the Ptolemaic epicycles that astronomers used to explain the apparent irregularity of planetary orbits, before the time of Kepler. However, if a typology can be constructed to include the routes of possible transition from one type to another, then one has a basis for limited predictions about future developments of different types of social systems, though this is a far cry from the grand evolutionary typologies of the nineteenth century.

Including routes of possible change in a typology enables one to compare what is changing, and what stays the same when a social unit undergoes transition from one type to another. When Durkheim (1897) attributed rising suicide rates to a decline in social norms, there was nothing to prevent a Bongo-Bongoist from countering his assertions by pointing to the emergence of new norms (a sort of diachronic Bongo-Bongoism). Our plan of resolving the dispute would be to measure changes in societies' rules systems over time. In other words, our quantification of grid/group analysis yields a typology of social change.

Perhaps most importantly, grid/group analysis enables us to analyze cultural values and beliefs as carefully maintained regulators of social organization, rather than as mere reflections of the economic or political order. Through grid/group analysis, we are able to see how symbols are invoked by people in order to convince and coerce each other to behave in a certain way, as well as to justify their own actions. Grid/group analysis shows how culture works as a social control mechanism and a means of accounting for actions. It explicitly classifies the strategies of disputants in familiar types of debates by showing how various arguments in families, churches, political parties, and sports clubs involve the fundamental issues of where the institution should draw its group boundary, and how it should regulate itself internally. Such endless debates about admission, penalties and remission, leadership styles and allocation of resources, all draw upon the protagonists' conceptions of the cosmos, of what is fair, what is possible, and above all, what is natural or even holy. The task for grid/group analysis is to identify the moral bias that arises in each kind of social organization.

This is not cultural determinism. It does not mean that individuals can only see the world one particular way according to their experience of grid/group pressures. The grid/group model does not preclude psychological theories of how different personality types might gravitate towards one kind of social context or another. It does not tell us what economic inducements or deprivations dispose persons to change their social organization and adapt their cosmological outlook accordingly. What grid/group analysis does assume, however, is first, that cultural bias is unavoidable and second, that there is a limited number of cultural packages from which people are free to choose when they settle for any particular style of social organization. Grid/group analysis indicates the path by which, of the many potential persons one might be at birth, one becomes one kind of person or another.

All anthropologists make the sorts of comparisons we are describing here. However, they usually make them at lower levels of formality. Although there are those who would be reluctant to associate their work with any typological approach, and especially one like ours that uses numerical scales, their own generalizations from synchronic or diachronic comparison involves, at the very least, an implicit informal typology.

We would argue that explicit comparisons are better, because they are more readily accessible to the scrutiny of others than implicit assumptions tucked away in the corners of an ethnographer's undeclared viewpoint. We prefer to devise explicit typologies, subject to the risk that they can be criticized and improved by others, than to preserve some misguided sense of humanistic integrity by sidestepping the problem of the relation between thought and society.

CHAPTER TWO

A CASE STUDY
VIEWPOINTS ON RISK IN
A NEW ENGLAND TOWN

To spotlight the basic aspects of grid/group analysis, we have
fabricated a case study, in which a hypothetical community is
seriously divided over the acceptability of having a nuclear
power plant located nearby. We have designed this example to
illustrate the different kinds of argumentation that might be
adopted in the different quadrants of the grid/group diagram.

2.1 This Example is Fictitious

What may be a novelty to some nonmathematicians is that the
example is not a real case study. We have invented an example
rather than describe a real one because our objective in this book
is to present a paradigm.

Why a Toy Example?

The examination of a toy problem is a familiar expository device in applied mathematics because many readers prefer gener-
alizing from a well-chosen example to particularizing from
abstractions. Thought experiments (Gedankenexperimenten)
have a long and honorable history in the natural sciences, especially physics. They have been used there in the early stages of a
field's development to ensure that costly and time-consuming
data-gathering efforts are undertaken only after there is some

assurance that even perfect data would, in fact, be able to illuminate the theory under investigation. Thought experiments are a way of asking whether the data would help us with understanding if we could gather them—a question surely as relevant to the social as to the natural sciences.

In this case, a real example would raise a host of potentially distracting questions about whether its particular analysis was based on an accurate interpretation of the actual events. As we are resolved that this remain a methodological treatise, we prefer to sidestep these issues, which inevitably arise in real ethnography.

It is also unlikely that a real example would present us with the opportunity to pay balanced attention to the whole range of cultural possibilities available on the grid/group diagram. Our example enables us to observe all four quadrants of the grid/group diagram. Moreover, a toy example enables us to concentrate on viewpoints that are nearly prototypical. In real social units there are often conflicts and inconsistencies of viewpoint that obscure the picture.

Of course, our example has not been conjured out of thin air. The core of our description is what journalists refer to as *composite story*, loosely based on real social units known from various locations. Readers familiar with the history of antinuclear campaigns in the United States may recognize certain similarities between the intervenor group we describe in the following pages and Johnsrud's description (1977) of Pennsylvania's Environmental Coalition on Nuclear Power.

The *Scallopshell Caucus*, featured in our example, owes more than just its name to the Clamshell and Abalone alliances. These militant antinuclear organizations have received extensive press coverage for their disobedience activities at Seabrook in New Hampshire and Diablo Canyon in California respectively (Douglas and Wildavsky 1982). We have also drawn upon the description of European counterparts to these groups given by Nelkin and Pollack (1980).

We have created a *Chamber of Commerce* and a *Trade Union Local* that more or less correspond to Thompson's descriptions

(1980, 1981) of the sort of hierarchical organizations that tend to favor nuclear energy. The responses of actual trade unionists to nuclear energy have been reported by Logan and Nelkin (1980), but our union has received the same degree of fictitious embellishment as the other units that we describe. Thus what follows is truly a simulated example and not simply a disguised description of any actual organizations or events.

2.2 A Power Plant Comes to Lakemouth

Our story concerns the small New England coastal town of Lakemouth (figure 2.1). Once an important commercial fishing center, it is still the principal town of the sizable rural county that shares its name.

Unfortunately, during the last thirty years, Lakemouth has suffered serious economic setbacks. An important contributor to Lakemouth's woes was the decline in consumption of fresh fish, due in part to relaxation of the Catholic Church's rule of Friday abstinence from meat.

The town's fishing industry was also adversely affected by changes in the demands for processed fish. For many years, much of the catch brought in by Lakemouth's owner-operated boats had been bought up by the local fish processing and canning plant. The plant was eventually forced to close, a victim of the increasing popularity of frozen fishsticks in the convenience food market. For a variety of technological and economic reasons, Lakemouth was not a competitive supplier for this new market.

The closure of the Lakemouth Canning Corporation was directly responsible for a jump in local unemployment, particularly among the women and the older workers who were not employed on the boats. The fishermen, too, were further affected by the loss of sales in this important local market.

Boat owners eventually took to hiring out their craft to visiting deep-sea anglers. The local Chamber of Commerce did everything possible to expand the town's tourist trade, which had been previously confined to a few foliage gazers attracted each fall to the extensive deciduous forest to the west of Lakemouth. However, despite these efforts to develop tourism, young people continued to migrate from the town to seek better opportunities elsewhere.

Thus, after three decades of unremitting decline, civic leaders were overjoyed when Coastal Gas and Electric (CG&E) proposed locating a large nuclear generating facility on the south

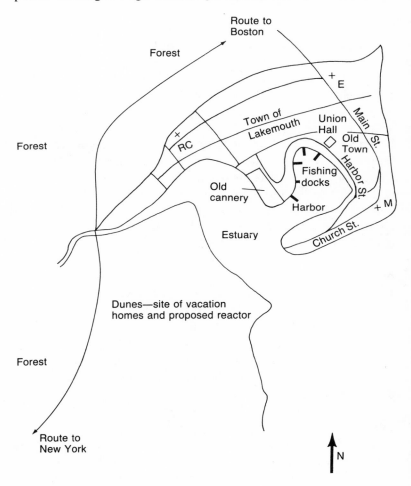

Figure 2.1. Lakemouth

shore of Lakemouth's estuary opposite the town. They were confident that it would stimulate the local economy by providing ample power for rejuvenating light industry in the area.

2.3 Support for the Plant

From its own past experience in trying to locate another nuclear power plant and from the experience of other utilities, Coastal Gas and Electric knew that it would be hard to predict how the local population would line up for and against their proposal.

The Chamber of Commerce

Accordingly, CG&E was delighted when the Chamber of Commerce endorsed the proposal. The members of the C of C were largely the merchants who owned the stores on Main Street, plus a small assortment of other established citizens. They had convened five times before taking a stand.

The winning argument at the Chamber of Commerce meetings was that the town could not withstand even another five years of migration of its young adults. If revival came too late, then when it did come it would bring an excess of outsiders who would have little respect for the pleasant ways of the present town. The opposition within the C of C took the position that Lakemouth is a New England fishing town, and that locating a nuclear power plant there would destroy its image, and with that image, the life the townspeople had always known. After a final straw vote at the fifth meeting showed predominant support for the plant, the members who had been in opposition agreed to lend their names to the statement of support.

Local 387

CG&E had made a serious mistake in its presentation of the proposal to General Workers Union Local 387, the main labor union in Lakemouth. What CG&E emphasized was a promise to give preference and training, if necessary, to local workers.

"You can tell Mr. Coastal, or whoever your boss is, that the issue is whether we will get cancer while you count your money," shouted one worker. "Besides that, tell him we want normal, healthy children."

It was difficult to blame the public relations staff of CG&E for this setback. In the town of their existing nuclear plant, they had started out telling the workers about risk, but the workers there had been more concerned that all of the jobs would go to outsiders.

While the leadership at Local 387 thought that their suspicions of these smooth talkers in expensive suits were well-founded, they were accustomed to negotiating with persons whose motives they did not trust. The leaders of Local 387 called the central offices of the General Workers Union for information.

They learned two important things. First, an engineering consultant and a physician hired by the GWU had both advised that, over the initial five-year period, the kind of plant proposed by CG&E was the safest kind known. Unfortunately, there were no data on long-term exposure to workers in such a plant. Second, CG&E was regarded by the parent union as a rather benevolent employer, a trifle too paternalistic, but willing to negotiate sensitive issues.

To a second meeting with the membership of Local 387, CG&E sent two officers of the union at its existing nuclear plant and a corporate vice-president in shirt sleeves who introduced himself as "Fred." One member of Local 387 joked, "These guys will try anything." It scarcely mattered, since Local 387 had already voted before the second meeting to endorse the plant. The beer and steamed clams served by CG&E were excellent.

T. R. Prendle

CG&E also received a letter of support from a Mr. T. R. Prendle, a gentleman farmer and large landowner. Prendle's letter stressed the absolute right of anyone to buy a piece of land and to do as he pleased with it. He criticized the company for asking the opinions of the town residents, and said that if they didn't get on with it, he might withdraw his support. Mr. Prendle was a person who wrote to the town newspaper regularly to express his views. At one time he had attended town meetings, but he stopped that after one session at which it became painfully clear that he was unlikely to persuade many persons of his opinions.

Children of Jupiter

There was some slight concern from CG&E about support expressed by the Children of Jupiter, a Boston-based doomsday cult. The Children of Jupiter always favored nuclear plants in the hope that a major disaster would convince additional persons of the imminence of doomsday.

The Dunes Dwellers

The only opposition which CG&E anticipated was from the well-to-do owners of a few expensive modern vacation homes among the sand dunes immediately adjacent to the proposed reactor site. Since the owners of these homes mainly lived in Boston and New York City, and used them only in the summer months, the utility anticipated that any opposition from these quarters could be overcome by generous compensation. Such compensation was mentioned immediately, and there was in fact no protest from the dunes dwellers.

The reaction of the dunes dwellers was so uniformly muted that one could imagine they had agreed on a common course of action. Despite the fact that families on the dunes had little contact with each other, it was plausible that they had reached consensus on the nuclear plant, because of a condominium-like deed restriction on dunes lots that bound their decisions together in this instance.

2.4 Opposition to the Plant

However, opposition to the utility sprung from an unexpected source, even while the dunes dwellers were surprisingly silent. Concern was voiced in parts of the town about the safety aspects of nuclear power.

Lakemouth Against Nuclear Energy (LANE)

An *ad hoc* organization, Lakemouth Against Nuclear Energy (LANE) sprang up in opposition to the plans to locate a reactor nearby. Its members cited the possibility of a catastrophic accident and the effects on the townspeople of continued exposure to low-level radiation. Fears were also expressed by members of LANE, who were mainly housewives, professional and recently retired people, that the town's tourist income would be adversely affected by the nuclear power plant.

LANE's activities included lobbying local and state politicians, and litigation to prevent compulsory sale of property or change of land use. Most importantly, LANE prepared a legal challenge against the plant to be brought before the licensing hearings scheduled by the Nuclear Regulatory Commission (NRC).

The activities of LANE brought the proposed Lakemouth reactor to the attention of the highly respected and long established National Wilderness Association. This association added its opposition to that of the local group because of what it perceived as the threat that the reactor would pose to the surrounding countryside, particularly to the ecology of the estuary, into which it would discharge its cooling water. As the National Wilderness Association did not have a significant local membership in Lakemouth, its role was principally as a technical adviser to LANE and as a registered intervenor at the licensing hearing.

However, even with the support of its national ally, LANE proved no match for the combined forces of the utility, the Chamber of Commerce, and the local trades unions, which argued forcefully to the NRC that the license should be granted. LANE responded to the NRC's decision that the reactor should be built by holding a public meeting at which its chairman announced his committee's intention to continue the fight through litigation on land use and access rights.

The Scallopshell Caucus

This course of action was not considered adequate by a vocal minority at the meeting. The dissidents argued that the institutions of judicial redress would be just as heavily biased in favor of the utility and the Chamber of Commerce as the regulatory agencies seemed to be. They accused LANE of being too soft in its opposition to the utility, and alleged that its leadership had shown a marked reluctance to upset personal friends, neighbors and business contacts among the powers that be in local politics and commerce.

Worst of all, claimed the minority, LANE had failed to identify the global scale of the nuclear menace. Simply to oppose the location of a nuclear power plant at Lakemouth conceded too much to the utility and its supporters. This limited course of opposition enabled the pro-nuclear forces to argue that since the plant had to be built somewhere, why should it not be at Lakemouth? After all, the town desperately needed the anticipated economic benefits.

No, said the dissidents, only a total, principled struggle against nuclear power, and against the military-industrial complex would stand a chance of success. No longer should opponents of the Lakemouth plant divert their energy into legal channels, which were expensive, time consuming, and insensitive to the democratic feelings of the population. In any case, the best that LANE's present strategy could achieve would be relocation of the plant a few miles further away. How far would it have to be not to threaten the citizens of Lakemouth, and anyway, was it not immoral to force someone else to live with the dangers that they would not accept for themselves?

LANE's leaders rebutted these criticisms, accusing the minority of wanting to expand the aims of the organization beyond the limits of practicality. Such a program of opposition to anything nuclear would, they argued, be divisive. It would embroil LANE in disarmament debates, line them up with pacifist groups, and lose LANE the support of many people who opposed the Lakemouth reactor, but felt differently about defense or even about other peaceful applications of the atom.

At the end of the meeting, the dissidents remained unconvinced by these arguments, and announced the formation of a new antinuclear group in the town, the Scallopshell Caucus. The founders of the caucus declared that their group would differ from LANE in three important respects.

First, it would be dedicated to total opposition to nuclear power throughout the state, and would attempt to link up with similar groups elsewhere to further its aims. Second, it would be democratic, unlike LANE, it would not rely on self-appointed retirees or professionals with the time and money to spare for intervening in hearings and litigation. Indeed, claimed the new group, it saw no need for officers at all. As it was everybody's struggle against the utility and the system which supported it, everyone should have an equal say in how that struggle should be waged.

Third, the Scallopshell Caucus would be dedicated to nonviolent direct action to prevent the Lakemouth reactor from being built. This would be public action aimed at involving large numbers of people, not just the few who were able to participate in NRC Hearings as registered intervenors, or could afford to take part in litigation. This direct action would include distributing leaflets, petitioning, holding rallies and fairs to publicize alternative energy sources, and nonviolent civil disobedience, such as blocking access roads to the reactor site, and even physical occupation of the site itself.

Jack Loveland

In addition to LANE and the Scallopshell Caucus, there were also individuals who opposed the plant. The most vocal of these was Jack Loveland, a real estate dealer, whose reasons for opposition were unclear, since he seemed to be one of the persons who would be generously compensated by CG&E.

Loveland was a licensed broker, but not the kind that shows homes to buyers. Instead he had made a fortune in timely purchases and sales of land. One of his poker-playing friends said, "Every opinion that Jack has is another dollar in his wallet."

2.5 A Speculative Review of the Dispute

Thus the lines were drawn for a complex and protracted dispute among the people of Lakemouth. The surprising thing to some was that these sides were not the familiar ones of party politics. The plans to build the power plant proposed by Coastal Gas and Electric had received active support and lobbying from the Chamber of Commerce and the local trades-union leaders. Since the Chamber of Commerce was staunchly Republican and the trades union members were predominantly Democrats, it was unusual for them to be on the same side of a political issue.

Opposition to the plan was forthcoming from two locally based groups, each having a markedly different style of opposition. LANE was a classic example of what students of planning controversies have christened a *nimby* (not-in-my-back-yard).

LANE was concerned primarily to prevent the construction of a nuclear reactor in Lakemouth. It did not extend its vision to curtailing the development of nuclear power elsewhere. LANE's chosen battlegrounds were the town council, the NRC licensing hearing and, if necessary, the courtroom. Its membership, like its interests and campaigning strategy, was purely localized. Members were, in many cases, acquainted with the local businessmen and civic leaders who were arguing in favor of the reactor. The sole support which LANE either sought or received from outside of Lakemouth, was the technical and legal advice of the well-respected conservation society, the National Wilderness Association, whose objection to the reactor was also to its location in an area of outstanding natural beauty and because of its effects on a delicate estuarial ecology.

The second opposition group was the Scallopshell Caucus, which was founded apparently as a reaction to LANE's initial defeat at the NRC hearing. This group was much more far-reaching in its campaign demands than LANE. It argued for all out opposition to nuclear power wherever it may be proposed.

The Scallopshell Caucus saw the hazards of the Lakemouth reactor as being greater than a local ecological disturbance, a statistical increase in cancer deaths, or a ruined tourist trade. It conjured up visions of a catastrophic accident that would turn the region into a latter day Hiroshima or Nagasaki. The Scallopshell Caucus disparaged the nice-guy tactics adopted by LANE, as well as its narrow localized vision of the problem. The caucus linked up with other groups in the state and in neighboring ones, and invited the members of these similar organizations to join its nonviolent activities to disrupt directly construction of the plant.

2.6 Challenges to the Cultural Analyst

Patterns of support and opposition to the nuclear power plant like those among the people of Lakemouth present a number of interesting challenges to the cultural analyst. First, one might ask if the alignments are simply based on perceived economic self-interest. In particular, the businessmen and the trades-unionists want new industry and new jobs respectively, while retired folk, professional people, and those who rely on the town's tourist trade see their property values and livelihoods threatened.

However, even if it were true that economic factors determined attitudes to the nuclear power plant in Lakemouth, one would still face a range of important questions about how the traditional adversaries of business and labor managed to bury their differences and to present a united position on this issue. For example, do the businessmen and trades-unionists have the same perception of the risks they are accepting along with nuclear power, and what kinds of strategies do they adopt to deal with the risks?

If one takes socioeconomic class, rather than crude self-inter-

of social units, not of persons. It is not a psychological theory of personality types, even though it has implications for such a theory.

It would be poor ethnography to compare individuals such as Prendle and Loveland directly with social units consisting of many individuals. As our discussion progresses it will become clear that we do not and cannot claim that every member of a social unit in a particular quadrant will exhibit a predictable attitude to any single issue, such as nuclear power. The existence of opposition within the Chamber of Commerce to the power plant is one indication that statistical variation is to be expected.

3.2 Assigning the Proponents To Their Quadrants

Let us now examine the factions that support the power plant and the different kinds of arguments they each mustered in its favor. Using only the theoretical foundations established by Douglas, we shall make a preliminary assignment of the disputants to grid/group quadrants, according to purely qualitative criteria. Subjective assessments of the relative frequency of personal interactions and of the strictness of membership requirements will be used to assess group strength. Impressions of hierarchical consistency or interchangeability of roles will be used to evaluate high or low grid strength. In chapter 6, our preliminary assignments will be tested (and verified) by a precise data analysis.

The Chamber of Commerce

The most ardent supporters of the power plant in the town of Lakemouth were almost certainly the members of the Chamber of Commerce, an organization that has long preserved many features of an exclusive club. Its membership consists of around fifteen persons, one-third being elected annually for overlapping three-year terms. Only continuing members can vote in these elections. Therefore, the C of C is largely self-perpetuating.

The Chamber of Commerce makes no attempt to represent all of the traders and shopkeepers in the town of Lakemouth, but draws on the support of only the thirty or so of the town's leading businessmen. Of these, most do not find themselves elected for continuous membership. There is rather an unofficial core of permanent members, and a minority of seats that are allowed to rotate among those remaining eligible for election. The Chamber's exclusiveness is demonstrated by the fact that in the year with which we are concerned, there were twenty eligible nonmembers, only three of whom were elected. This low ratio of the number of new members to potential members indicates a high group style or organization.

Another important indication of high group strength is the range of activities in which members of the Chamber of Commerce collectively participate. In addition to the regular monthly meetings to discuss the commercial and political affairs of Lakemouth, the members organize a variety of social events for their families. They regularly hold barbecues in the summer and cocktail parties in the winter months, in one or another member's home.

The Chamber also organizes a number of events open to the whole population of the town, but whose planning involves only the members and their wives (women are seldom elected as members). These events include the town's Fourth of July celebrations, the annual Summer Fair and Flower Show, the Thanksgiving Charity Ball, the town's Christmas festivities (including street illuminations, Santa's procession, and the like), and the Easter Parade.

The Chamber is predominantly Episcopalian, so most members attend the same church. They and their families meet for services and other church events. Similarly, the predominance of Republican affiliations also ensures that Chamber of Commerce members interact frequently in local politics. This extensive range of activities ensures the involvement of all of the members of the Chamber, their wives, and children in the affairs of the Chamber. The intensity of these activities guarantees that everyone involved in the Chamber of Commerce will interact frequently with each other, and that they are able to devote relatively little time to outside activities. All of these factors serve to reinforce the impression that the Chamber of Commerce is a high-group organization.

So far as grid characteristics are concerned, the Chamber of Commerce seems to exhibit a strong differentiation of roles. The members themselves distinguish between permanent members and those who are elected for single terms, although this distinction is not acknowledged in the Chamber's written constitution. There are also formal roles set down in the constitution for a chairman, a president, a secretary, a treasurer, and a social secretary. Further division of roles exists between the chairmen and members of various standing committees, which exist to advise the Chamber on financial and commercial affairs. Moreover, there are *ad hoc* organizing committees for the various large scale social events which the Chamber sponsors. Wives and families of members also serve on the social committees. but they are not involved in the business activities of the Chamber.

External status is also acknowledged within the Chamber and it may profoundly affect the chance that a particular individual attains office within the organization. Principal officers of the Chamber are invariably selected from among the older members. The occupation of a member is the primary factor that determines who becomes a permanent member and who is considered eligible only for a rotating seat.

The extensive division of responsibility for organizing the diverse activities of the Chamber of Commerce and the separation of roles attached to specific offices within each activity are both indicative of a high-grid form of social organization. A qualitative grid/group analysis would therefore place the Chamber of Commerce firmly within quadrant C as a high-grid/high-group social unit.

Union Local 387

Local 387 also seems to exhibit high-group characteristics, although it is much less exclusive than the Chamber of Commerce.

The GWU has not sought to establish a closed shop, but it has actively recruited unskilled and semiskilled workers. Of the 240 workers in Lakemouth's GWU shops, only 20 have chosen not to join Local 387. Membership in the GWU is a simple matter of enrollment and paying dues. There are no grades of membership like the unofficial permanent and rotating memberships of the Chamber of Commerce. Once admitted, the union member need only pay his dues to keep all of the privileges of membership.

Despite its lack of exclusiveness, the union local shares some of the high-group features of the Chamber of Commerce. The union organizes a wide range of political and social activities for its members. The local union hall is an important meeting place where members may gather any of six nights a week to drink and socialize. Lakemouth has no public movie theater at present, so the Union Hall film show for members' families is a popular Wednesday night event.

The union also organizes summer picnics and barn dances in the winter months, which provide frequent opportunities for members and their families to meet. Evening classes in a variety of topics are also held at the union hall under the sponsorship of Local 387. Although those are also open to nonmembers, it is mainly unionists and their families who make good use of this facility during the long winter evenings.

Churchgoing is less regular among unionists than among members of the Chamber of Commerce. There is a preponderance of Methodists and Roman Catholics among union members, many of whom therefore interact in church activities in addition to those of their union. This wide range of common activities serves to reinforce the extensive contact of union members in their places of work, to produce a relatively high-group environment. However, the lack of exclusiveness indicates that Local 387 is not quite so high-group as the Chamber of Commerce.

Local 387 is also similar to the Chamber of Commerce in that its wide variety of activities provides members with the opportunity to take on one or more distinctive specialized roles, which is typical of a high-grid environment. The local is run by an elected executive committee consisting of the best established activists. Although there are some younger members, the average age of executive committee members is about ten years over that of the whole local. The committee consists of a president, a chairman, a secretary, a treasurer, a membership officer, a social and welfare secretary (usually the token woman's position on the executive), an education officer (who runs the evening classes), and eight ordinary members who serve as deputies to one or another of the titled executive officers.

In addition, there are standing committees for educational, political, financial and social affairs and also for welfare services. Each standing committee consists of two or more ex-officio members from the executive, and about five other members of the local, elected at the annual general meeting, or selected by the subcommittee itself, subject to the approval of the executive committee. *Ad hoc* committees are appointed from time to time, largely to provide extra labor for organizing events such as barn dances and rummage sales.

Although probably the division of roles is less rigid than in the Chamber of Commerce, Local 387 still exhibits a considerable degree of role specialization and hierarchy. This establishes it as a high-grid social unit. Local 387 can therefore be assigned to quadrant C, but somewhat closer to the center of the diagram than the Chamber of Commerce.

The Dunes Dwellers

Each of the seven gaudy vacation homes nestling among the dunes is situated well apart from the others. They are owned by prosperous businessmen from New York and Boston who, despite their public silence, seem to be supporters of the nuclear plant.

In the height of the summer, the dunes community seems deceptively large, because family friends and business associates of the dunes dwellers are often invited for the weekend, or sometimes for a week during the school holidays. Thus, there are numerous transient residents at the dunes, in addition to the permanent core of homeowning families.

An important consequence of the house-party pattern of social organization at the dunes is that it is often difficult to determine who the permanent occupants really are. Only by carefully observing the weekend crowds at neighboring houses over several weeks is it possible to guess who is the actual homeowner and who are the guests. This task is particularly difficult at two houses whose owners do not come every weekend, but send their own children to the dunes in care of family friends.

Since the houses are so far apart and since each house is the center of its own social activities, there is very little occasion for social interaction between households. Members of different weekending parties sometimes greet each other with casual friendliness on the beach or on the boardwalks that connect the houses to the road. However, the separate parties tend to remain separate, and there is very seldom any but the briefest contact between one house and another.

There are serious difficulties in identifying changes in membership of the dunes community, so it is hard to appraise the relative strength or weakness of its group boundary. It is difficult even to establish the size of the community. Do we count frequent visitors, or just the families of homeowners?

A good case could be made here for counting just the individual owners of the properties. After all, the influence of spouses and children in deciding about property disposal might vary uncontrollably from family to family. No matter how we overcome these particular problems, we anticipate difficulty in finding empirical criteria by which to define a social unit when the group strength is this low. The homeowners barely know each other. They invite continually changing entourages to their separate houses for a very limited range of significant activities, all of which could be lumped under the rubric of "hanging out by the sea."

The dunes dwellers also exhibit low-grid characteristics. There is no formally defined organization, such as a residents' association. Administrative decisions about road maintenance and other such matters are left to a local real estate manager. Thus the possibility of formal office holding within the community does not arise. Within the individual households, roles are seldom well-defined, and those that can be detected are often transitory and interchangeable. Even the roles of host and guest are ambiguous. Guests often bring liquor and prepare cocktails in the evenings, or else they will bring food and cook for their hosts in an informal reversal of their roles as guests.

The competitiveness that we anticipate in low-grid/low-group environments is evident in the speedboats beached on trailers by each house. The latest status-conferring leisure toy—one year a dune buggy, the next year a windsurf board—spreads from one house to another in the course of a summer season, only to be supplanted by something yet more exciting and fashionable the following year.

The occupational characteristics of the dunes dwellers are further evidence that their role behavior at Lakemouth is a transplantation of their low-grid social organization from the city. The homeowners are self-made entrepreneurs, supersalesmen, or executives in highly competitive industries.

The ostentatious life of the dunes has not attracted established wealthy families. This is not the playground of old money but of the *nouveau riche*. The dunes dwellers achieved their wealth neither through inheritance nor through working in a conservative bureaucracy. These are upwardly mobile, highly motivated individualists. They are not members of clearly defined networks, but rather, persons who pick and choose their associates as it suits them. They blur the distinction between business and pleasure at the dunes, to which the frequent appearance of business associates among the guests will testify. The dunes community is a clear case of a quadrant A social environment.

Were it not for complications in their deeds, it is unthinkable that this collection of persons would act in unison. One would expect a flurry of tricks and private deals in which each seeks to do as well as possible for himself. Although these people would not mind leaving their neighbors in the lurch, they are capable of making quick deals with each other. Such flexibility is likely to be a contributing factor to their material success.

3.3 **Quadrants for the Various Opponents**

The initial focus of opposition to the Lakemouth reactor came from LANE, the largely makeshift organization of housewives, professionals, and retired persons. Membership of LANE is very informal. Anyone who comes to meetings, signs a petition, or is involved in the campaign is counted as a member. Since there are no subscriptions or formal memberships, and since the intensity of many of the campaigners' involvement in LANE activities fluctuates, the size of LANE is difficult to determine. Similarly, the number of potential members is hard to gauge, because the only criterion for admission is opposition to the power plant. There is no waiting list of members. Therefore, any resident of the Lakemouth vicinity who expresses misgivings about the plant could be counted as a potential member.

For the purposes of this study, membership was determined to be those individuals associated with LANE who devote time to its activities on a regular weekly basis for a sustained period. On this basis LANE numbers 41 members. There is a much larger number of occasional supporters.

However, the *ad hoc* nature of the group and its continually varying population suggest a low-group condition. High-group organizations usually establish unambiguous criteria for membership and demand constant support from their members.

The impression of low-group organization is confirmed by the restricted range of activities engaged in by LANE. These are wholly confined to campaigning activities such as writing letters, preparing petitions, distributing handbills, and engaging in litigation against the utility company. LANE does not provide its members with a broad spectrum of social activities of the sort laid on by either the Chamber of Commerce or Local 387. The fundraising activities of Lane are confined to requesting donations for expenses like printing costs from persons who sign the organization's petitions or attend its public meetings.

Most LANE members seldom see each other outside of their campaigning context. Some of the professional members of LANE live in outlying areas. Many of those who both live and work in Lakemouth are professionals who have little day-to-day contact with each other. Many of the older members of LANE have moved to Lakemouth after their retirement from work and have not established strong ties with each other or with the local community.

Lakemouth housewives are more often than not mothers of schoolchildren, and they have relatively little social life outside of child-centered activities like school events or sports leagues. This fragmentation of LANE's membership and the absence of recreational and other social contacts contributes to LANE's distinctly low-group character by comparison with the Chamber of Commerce or Local 387. However, LANE does seem to merit a higher group rating than the highly individualistic dunes dwellers.

LANE depends almost entirely on external status for its internal allocation of roles. There is a largely self-appointed coordinating committee chaired by a local lawyer, who is also the organization's principal legal representative. The treasurer is a junior officer of the First National Bank of Lakemouth. The committee's secretary and publicist is a retired journalist from the Boston Globe. The remaining members of the coordinating committee are a schoolteacher, an architect, and a housewife, who is also the only independent member of the town council. Since the occupancy of organization offices is largely based on prior statuses and skills, there is little opportunity for turnover.

About fifteen young mothers, college dropouts, and teenage activists are in LANE. They are expected to carry out a variety of relatively routine tasks, such as door-to-door signature collection for petitions, writing out letters to local politicians and newspapers according to the formula suggested by the committee, and passing the hat around at public meetings. However, even these roles tend to be specialized. For instance, one person is a reliable door-to-door canvasser, but unwilling (or perhaps inept) to write letters.

The status differential between committee members and activists was precisely one of the bones of contention raised by the founders of the Scallopshell Caucus. These breakaways resented what they perceived as their exclusion from any directional activity, all of which was conducted by an elite core of already privileged individuals who sought to preserve their own interests and property values by having the reactor sited elsewhere. Based on its system of role allocation, we discern a high-grid condition in LANE, though probably not so high as the Chamber of Commerce. Since LANE is low group, our net assessment locates LANE in quadrant B, the environment of stratified individuals with relatively weak incorporation into a social network.

The Scallopshell Caucus

The Scallopshell Caucus presents a markedly different picture from LANE in almost every respect. The caucus numbers about half as many members as LANE. Membership is more clearly defined because new recruits are required to take an oath of allegiance to the environment, in which they pledge to defend natural resources and to oppose nuclear power and other threatening technologies whenever and wherever they arise. The oath is brief and informally administered, usually in the open air. However, it signifies the full incorporation of a new member into the organization. The membership is precisely defined as the set of 19 activists who have taken the oath.

Scallopshell activities are numerous and wide-ranging. The membership is largely younger than LANE's and certainly more energetic. The Scallops have organized a variety of visible protests against the plant. These include an antinuclear street theater, a symbolic occupation of the reactor site on the anniversary of the Hiroshima and Nagasaki bombings, and harassment of initial survey teams sent by CG&E to prepare detailed plans for the site.

Unlike members of LANE, Scallopshell members do not have access to private funds to pay for their organizational costs. They therefore organize a variety of fundraising activities, which have included the First Lakemouth Alternative Energy Festival. This event featured exhibits of all kinds of ingenious solutions to the problems of energy production by individuals and small commercial concerns from all over the country. The festival also included performances by a number of folk singers and musicians of local prominence and the appearance of a nationally known recording star famous for his opposition to nuclear power.

Rummage sales, street collections, and a newspaper recycling scheme have all involved the Scallopshell Caucus in a high level of intense activity. All of these events are organized by the caucus as a whole, and responsibilities are not subdivided among discrete committees or task forces. This leads to a high frequency of face-to-face contacts among the membership, which is characteristic of a high-group environment. There is a constant linkage of social events and fundraising activity, which seems to indicate that Scallops do not separate their social lives from their involvement in the caucus. In fact, for most Scallops, the caucus is their social life, and even during brief respites from group activities Scallopshell members will choose to spend their leisure time with other group members. All of these factors point to a high-group consciousness.

The absence of committees, and the full sharing of organizational tasks by the whole membership are indicative of low grid. There is a conspicuous absence of specialized roles, hierarchies, and other internal status distinctions. We may recall that when the Scallopshell Caucus was launched, the founders specifically attacked LANE for its undemocratic organization. In contrast, the Scallops set up a communitarian form of organization in which everybody does everything. By abjuring specialization, they hoped to preempt the appropriation of power by officeholders, or the establishment of publicly recognized leaders who might be persuaded to compromise by the utility, or incorporated into the establishment by the shirt-sleeved corporate vice-presidents of CG&E. Our overall impression of the Scallopshell Caucus is of a quadrant D type of organization, the high-group/low-grid environment of tightly knit egalitarians.

The Overall Spread

Overall, the social units supporting or opposing the Lakemouth reactor are spread over the grid/group diagram as shown in figure 3.1. Those supporting the reactor are to be found at diagonally

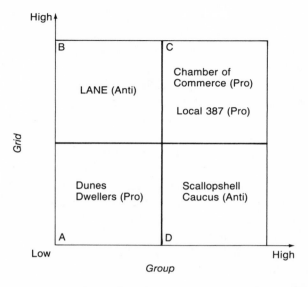

**Figure 3.1. Assignment of Lakemouth social units to grid/group
quadrants according to qualitative assessments
of their organizational structure**

opposite corners of the diagram, the dunes dwellers in quadrant
A (low grid/low group) and the Chamber of Commerce and Local
387 in quadrant C (high grid/high group). The opponents of the
reactor are also to be found at diagonally opposite corners of the
diagram. The local nimby, LANE, is assigned to quadrant B
(high grid/low group) while the Scallopshell Caucus seems to fit
nicely into quadrant D (low grid/high group).

We are conscious that in assigning LANE to quadrant B we
are taking issue with Douglas and Wildavsky's contention that
quadrants A, C, and D are sufficient to describe all public controversy about risk. We agree that quadrant B folk are likely to have
fewer resources to participate than entrepreneurs, bureaucrats or
egalitarians (with their dedicated stock of human capital). But,
this tendency does not absolutely exclude them from possible
participation. We feel that our characterization of this nimby as
high grid/low group, quite distinct from the egalitarians of low
grid/high group, is also more consistent with ethnographic de-

scriptions of localized opposition movements (Johnsrud 1977; Sorensen et al. 1983).

From the events at Lakemouth, it would be tempting to generalize that social units with quadrant A (low/low) or quadrant C (high/high) patterns always favor nuclear plants and that those with quadrant B (high/low) or quadrant C (low/high) patterns invariable oppose them. Reality is not this simple, for two main reasons.

First, we have already made the point that we expect normal statistical variation with respect to the distribution of a cosmology throughout each of the social units. That is, our model asserts tendencies, not certainties. There was, for example, initial opposition to the power plant within both the Chamber of Commerce and Local 387, which eventually became its most ardent advocates. Opposing members of each organization may have given way to the majority, but it is unlikely that they are uniformly favorable in their opinions.

Our need to be aware of statistical variation is emphasized by the fact that, had we not excluded single individuals from our example, we would have allocated T. R. Prendle, who favored the project, to high grid/low group, alongside LANE. Conversely, we would have assigned Jack Loveland, who opposed the project, to low grid/low group along with the dunes dwellers who favored the plant.

The second factor that we must take into account when interpreting the distributions of attitudes toward the Lakemouth power plant across the grid/group diagram is that although we can predict that social units from any single quadrant will have a similar cosmological sensitivity to risk in general, their attitudes toward any specific risk may vary according to additional influences.

Had Loveland stood to gain financially from the construction of the plant, as the dunes dwellers hoped to, we are sure that he would have reversed his position. Such pragmatism is a characteristic of low-grid/low-group behavior that prevents us from making a categorical linkage between this sort of social unit and its predominating attitude to nuclear power.

Similarly, had we included them in our analysis, we would have allocated the Children of Jupiter doomesday cult to quadrant D alongside the Scallopshell Caucus. But, while both have a consistent cosmological disposition toward prophesies of doom, the Scallops, not unreasonably, wish to avoid such a fate, while the Children of Jupiter for reasons that do not concern us here, would welcome disaster as evidence of the imminent fulfillment of their millennialist expectations.

Thus, it is to be expected that some social units will act counter to the mainstream. Even when statistically unlikely events occur, we do believe that our analysis can reliably detect a general cosmological bias in a social unit that will account for the kinds of justification that its members will marshal to support its arguments.

3.4 Cultural Bias For and Against the Lakemouth Reactor

This fictitious Lakemouth example illustrates the wide spread of organizational and cosmological variation that grid/group analysis can support. It is our contention that the fabricated correlation of grid/group position and attitudes toward the Lakemouth reactor would be likely to occur in the real case.

The fundamental principle of grid/group theory is that people structure their ideas about both the natural and social worlds in a way that is compatible with their experience of organizational structure in whatever social unit constitutes the main focus of their daily lives. Attitudes toward risk in general, and more particularly toward what kinds of risks are culturally acceptable are a function of how people in a given social unit understand the world and their place in it. Attitudes toward risk are an integral part of everyone's cultural bias.

The Dunes Dwellers

Our reason for attributing cultural bias in favor of the Lakemouth reactor to the dunes dwellers is precisely that these are people whose social experience is a risk-laden one. They are aggressive individualists who are unconstrained by loyalties to any clearly defined corporate group, and unregulated in their behavior by their position in a hierarchy, or other form of attributed social status. They are entrepreneurs who are accustomed to maintaining social networks from which they pick and choose with whom to interact according to their needs or desires of the moment. Their attitude toward the risks of nuclear technology in general is likely to be pragmatic. After all, they reason, none of the technological advances which have brought them the benefits of modern life have been achieved without risk. To those whose very existence depends upon innovation of one sort or another, acceptance of attendant risks is a necessary component of their world.

So far as the dunes dwellers' specific attitude toward the Lakemouth reactor is concerned, they have a particular stake in its construction. If the reactor is built, they probably stand to gain financially from CG&E's purchase of their property. Of course, CG&E might somehow manage to avoid purchasing the dunes properties, in which case those that remain would decline substantially in value. However, this is just one more risk that those entrepreneurs are prepared to incorporate into their investment portfolios.

Their individual judgments are that the odds are in their favor, that the reactor will be built, and that the utility company will purchase their properties. Support for nuclear energy, or any other purportedly high-risk technology is therefore, not a simple function of the entrepreneurial lifestyle. If the dunes dwellers perceived that the balance of probabilities was against their own interests, that they were likely to take a substantial loss on the value of their homes from the construction of the reactor on an adjacent site, we would expect them to engage in considerable wheeling and dealing to persuade the utility to move it elsewhere. In such an eventuality their battleground would know no bounds, and it is quite conceivable that they would join forces with LANE and even the Scallopshell Caucus if it suited their own ends.

There is another significant element in the low-grid/low-group cosmology that makes nuclear power more acceptable to the dunes dwellers than to some other inhabitants of Lakemouth. This element is a relatively short-term view of the future. The dunes dwellers are used to making short-term gains. They are not executives of bureaucratic corporations with a corporate life expectance far beyond that of any individual who works for them. Nor are they custodians of old money who plan for the future of family fortunes.

It is true that some dunes dwellers might later follow the example of their nineteenth-century predecessors and switch their efforts from the accumulation of fortunes to the consolidation of their economic and social success. In so doing, they would transform their life-styles and cosmologies according to the more cautious, long-term patterns of behavior suited to established institutions of the sort to be found in quadrant C. However, the dunes dwellers we know today are still quick-deal artists accustomed to meeting urgent deadlines, who are oriented toward the realization of investments in the short run. As such they are unlikely to be susceptible to cries that waste disposal may present problems to posterity. Future innovations will find ways of dealing with such problems, they reason optimistically, just as we have had to deal with the drawbacks inherited from the industrialism of previous generations. In general, the cultural bias of low-grid/low-group is toward the short term. Long-term prophecies of doom have little appeal in quadrant A.

The C of C and Local 387

But what about the Chamber of Commerce and Local 387? They have an experience of social organization diametrically opposed to that of the dunes dwellers. They are high grid/high group; why then do they not oppose the reactor and all the hazards it may present? Our answer is that the reasons for high-grid/high-group acceptance of the risks of nuclear power are quite different from those of the low-grid/low-group dunes dwellers.

There is a whole body of sociological literature to testify that bureaucrats and hierarchists are masterful creators of routines

(March and Simon 1958, Cyert and March 1963). In particular, high-grid/high-group people tend to cope with dangers by inventing standardized procedures that frequently include compensation for loss. Low-grid/low-group people, by way of contrast, tend to think that compensating the losers deprives the winners of incentive. The aim of bureaucracies is to systematize behavior as much as possible, and even to produce standard responses to the breakdown of procedures. Should the back-up measures fail, complex bureaucratic institutions will invoke standard procedures for inquiring into their failure, and so on.

In this kind of social environment, confidence in the institutions is an essential feature of the cosmology. Without it, the institutions themselves would not be viable. Local 387's referral of the nuclear hazard problem to its national headquarters is an example of such confidence. The risks to which high-grid/high-group persons are likely to be most sensitive are not technological hazards that can be mitigated by the development of stringent safety standards, but the social risks of lost confidence in the institutions that decide what is socially acceptable and what is not.

The Chamber of Commerce is clearly more concerned about the decay of Lakemouth's social institutions, brought on by economic decline, than about possible risks from nuclear power. In much the same way, Local 387 has come to worry about its own future unless Lakemouth's high unemployment levels can be reduced by the introduction of new light industry.

The temporal perception at high-grid/high group also supports acceptance of nuclear hazards. History here is the history of institutions that have been successful at coping with past problems. Prophecies of cataclysmic disasters have little credibility here provided that institutions are strong.

LANE's Cultural Bias

LANE's opposition to the Lakemouth reactor is equally predictable, and just as well supported by its members' social experience as the support for the project offered by the dunes dwellers, the Chamber of Commerce, and Local 387. The members of LANE are not members of supportive networks like those enjoyed by members of the high-grid/high-group units. Strongly constrained by their perceptions of their own social status, the members of LANE also lack the free-wheeling entrepreneurial resources of the low-grid/low-group dunes dwellers. Retired people, professionals, housewives, and teenagers do not have the political clout of trades-unionists or businessmen. They see themselves, rightly or wrongly, as the vulnerable sectors of society, the people things get done to, rather than the doers. Therefore, it is hardly surprising that these individuals feel especially threatened by decisions made by utility companies and politicians. Retired persons do not want the value of their small nest-egg retirement homes threatened by the proximity of a nuclear reactor. Housewives do not want their children exposed to possible genetic damage by the profit motives of anonymous corporations.

Opposition among the lower ranks in a quadrant B social unit to risk-bearing is highly personalized. It stems principally from a perceived inequity of risks, borne by themselves, and benefits, accruing to powerful others.

Time in quadrant B is perceived as endless and orderly. High-grid/low-group people are therefore less likely to be alarmed by cataclysmic tales of reactor disasters than they are to be sensitized to the possibilities of slow damage caused by radiation leakage, and to manipulations of their lives by others. Therefore, they do not share the global hostility towards all things nuclear that we identified within the Scallopshell Caucus. High-grid/low-group LANE just does not want a potentially dangerous technology foisted on it by someone else.

The Scallopshell Caucus

Last, we must interpret the opposition of the Scallopshell Caucus within a grid/group framework. Low grid/high group is the domain of egalitarians who do not accept the status differentiations that larger society would impose on them. Here, persons escape the straitjacket of social classification by banding together within a network of fellow souls to create their own common-wealth of equals.

Nuclear power is a capital-intensive energy source that can only be controlled by large corporations and centralized govern-ments. As such it is a symbol of the kind of society which low gridders/high groupers reject. This rejection of nuclear power is reinforced by the perception of time at low grid/high group. Or-ganizations of this sort lack institutional means of resolving dis-putes. Each member's viewpoint is as valuable as another's. There are no leaders and no procedures for unlocking stalemates when no consensus can be reached. Hence, these organizations are susceptible to schisms and tend to be short-lived. The Scal-lopshell Caucus was itself the product of a split from LANE when its founders' views were unable to prevail. Memories of the past, and projections into the future, therefore, tend to be compressed within these tight-knit units.

Scenarios of imminent catastrophe are therefore more credible in the quadrant D social environment than elsewhere. The Scal-lopshell Caucus' global opposition to any nuclear technology, whenever it may be found, is therefore a predictable cosmologi-cal outcome of its social structure.

3.5 Credibility of the Hypothesis

Thus far, we have produced an hypothesis that relates the organizational experience of Lakemouth's inhabitants to a dis-tinct cultural bias for or against nuclear power in general, and the Lakemouth reactor in particular. However, our grid/group anal-ysis is largely impressionistic and anecdotal. How could we set about testing such an hypothesis in a real case where we would have to face three serious objections to the sort of subjective qualitative assessments that we have made here?

First, there is the problem of selection. Might not another in-vestigator select different social units for analysis? How do we know that our selection is an appropriate one? Could we not expose the issues more clearly than we have done by cutting a different sort of slice into Lakemouth society? Even if we have selected the right units, might we arrive at very different assessments of their grid/group strength by emphasizing other aspects of their organization?

Second, there is the problem of replicability. How can we be sure that we are assessing the same things by the same yardstick when moving from one unit to another, or when assessing the same unit over time? Without some basis for objective measurement, different investigators might agree that they are examining the same criteria while disagreeing about the strength of grid or group that they indicate.

Finally, we face a problem of significance. Only by some sort of measurement can we tell whether the cosmological differences between two samples correspond to a significant quantitative difference between their grid/group strengths.

These problems can only be overcome by the introduction of a precisely definable model of the social unit to which grid/group analysis can be applied, and the development of scales for the measurement of variation in that model. Since no single criterion or set of criteria is appropriate to all social units or organizations, our model is polythetic, as explained in chapter 4. The model and scales are presented in chapter 5.

Obviously, grid/group analysis and other scientific methods do not relieve us of the burden (or joy) of philosophical debate. For instance, if someone thinks that our definition of, say, bureaucracy or competition, does not capture its true meaning, then we have an opportunity to argue meanings. However, it is wholly constructive to separate the empirical question of whether a given social unit has a specified property from the semantic problem of justifying a name for the property.

CHAPTER FOUR

POLYTHETIC SCALES
FOR GRID AND GROUP

In the previous chapter, we used a variety of subjectively assessed criteria to decide the relative grid/group strength of each body of disputants at Lakemouth. But, we did not consistently apply all of the criteria to every case. This is not unusual in social science. Historians and anthropologists often rely on experience and intuition to make qualitative assessments of a "more than" or "less than" nature. But, where consensus is absent, there is no way to resolve disputes about how much more or less of a given factor makes a significant difference to the way a society behaves or thinks, unless the basis for assessments is quantified.

The first difficulty encountered in trying to quantify grid/group analysis arises from the generality of the concepts of grid and group. The terms seem so broad, so all-embracing, that it appears difficult to isolate the sample features of concrete cases that we should be measuring. We need a workable procedure to decide at what point in the planar diagram a particular social unit should be represented.

What muddies the water is that those who have employed in the past the sort of qualitative assessments given in chapter 3 have actually interpreted grid and group in quite different ways, often without providing an explicit justification for them. For a selection of these interpretations see Douglas (1982).

However, this interpretive diversity—the selection of seemingly quite disconnected factors as indications of grid or group strength, as well as the variability of the criteria from case to case—need not be an obstacle to understanding the grid and group coordinates nor to measuring them. Indeed the diversity of factors serving as potential indicators is central to the concepts of grid and group as developed in this book. From our viewpoint, several diverse aspects of grid or group may be measured in various combinations, because both coordinates are polythetically constituted.

4.1 Explanation of Polythetic Classification

Polythetic classification is the formation of classes according to a number of characteristics, such that no single characteristic has to be present in every member of any class. The basic principles of this approach have been enunciated in the works of two of this century's leading philosophers, Gilbert Ryle (1949, 1951), who called it *polymorphous* classification, and Ludwig Wittgenstein (1953), who described it as classification by *family resemblances*. Polythetic classification has also been developed in the biological sciences, where there has been pervasive concern about the contradiction between apparently natural categories discovered by empirical observation and anomalous cases, such as fungi, which are unique among living species classified as plants in that they do not photosynthesize. Similar concepts have already been introduced into psychology and anthropology by Vygotsky (1962) and Needham (1975) respectively.

Polythetic classification is quite different from traditional *monothetic* classification, which defines a class by reference to a property that is necessary and sufficient for membership. By way of contrast a polythetic class is designed on the principle that individuals are assigned to a class according to a set of properties subject to the following general conditions: 1) Each individual possesses a large but unspecified proportion of the chosen properties; 2) Each property is more commonly found among individuals in the class than among individuals outside the class but in the same domain. It is not required that any property in the set must occur in every individual in the class.

Some persons, for example, Vygotsky (1962), view a polythetic category as a chain in which the number and combination of features forming the linkage changes from member to member. Of course, the full set of definitive features for the whole category must be specified. For unless the nature of the links is restricted, a chain with infinitely variable links could connect anything to any other thing, and would be of little use for defining a set. Subject to this restriction, it may happen that in a polythetically defined class, some members at opposite ends of the chain may hardly resemble each other at all, for no characteristic need be universally distributed.

Polythetic Scales

By a polythetic scale, we mean a possibly weighted combination of a number of separate indices, not all of which need be included as constituents. There is an obvious theoretical basis for defining polythetic scales for grid and group. Indeed, Hampton (1982) has already produced simple polythetic-type scales for grid/group analysis based on questionnaire responses about group membership and hierarchy. These scales were constructed in accordance with procedures commonly used for psychological test construction. The measures we are about to demonstrate are formulated at a more general level and exploit more of the formal features of polythetic classification.

When we say that the dimensions of grid and group are both polythetically constituted, we mean that there is no single item of empirical social behavior that must be present in every case for us to be able to measure either grid or group. In both a layman's sense and in ours, group commitment consists of a large number of factors, any or all of which may be present at varying strengths and in different combinations. Similarly, the extent of role differentiation, and controls over access to roles may also take a variety of forms. As neither group nor grid can be defined by a single omnipresent *essence* we may justifiably interpret them as polythetic concepts.

One motivation for adopting a flexible polythetic approach is that new knowledge can be utilized in applying polythetic concepts without the necessity of modifying the definitions and redrawing the boundaries of a class every time an anomaly arises. Furthermore, polythetic classification leaves the classifier free to choose from a wide range of possible variables, the particular combination of available elements that are of interest in the construction of a typology for whatever project is in hand.

No single property of a polythetic category can be said to provide the definitive or the most natural classification of its members. The fact that polythetic categories contain more explicit information than monothetic categories makes them not only eminently suitable for the construction of typologies based on the explicit special interests of the classifier, but also an excellent model for the constitution of the grid and group coordinates.

4.2 **The Necessity of Operational Predicates**

Defining grid or group on the basis of bundles of similar properties, all related to role distinctions or group commitments, leaves us with the problem of how to justify the limits of the bundle. Where do we draw the line and say that such-and-such a factor does not operate significantly as a grid or group type of social constraint?

Following Campbell (1965), Needham (1975) and others have argued that a polythetic category must have a list of what are called *basic predicates*. Rather than circumscribing the boundary of a category on the basis of shared characteristics, we interpret basic predicates as the principles that enable us to connect items in family resemblance chains. Predicates, therefore, are not empirical properties of the objects of classification, but are formal features of the classifier's model.

In biological classification, the concept of common descent is one such principle for the classification of species, and may be said to be one of the basic predicates of natural taxonomy. However, common descent is not an observable feature of particular individuals. It is a theoretical principle of the evolutionary model of living things.

The use of formal predicates rather than empirical properties as the basis of categories is, in itself, inimical to single-factor definitions of a class. Continuing the biological example, the theory of evolution does not tell us that common descent alone constitutes the essence of a species. One of Darwin's most important theoretical assertions was that various species of apes shared a common ancestor with Homo sapiens. Thus, common descent alone does not imply that two animals are of the same species. Beyond the fact that common descent may be part of a definition of all species, there is no reason to suppose that it is the one element which is definitive among a set of variables.

Polythetic classifications are really very familiar. In the formation of everyday classifications a basic predicate of a classificatory model may be proximity to a prototype. Other members of the class may deviate from a prototype while retaining sufficient family resemblances to be included in that class. For example, the prototype *chair* may be a dining chair to which armchairs, thrones, and car seats are compared by the classifier, in order to see whether they merit inclusion in the category of chairs (Hampton 1979). However, the principle of proximity to a prototype is not alone sufficient to constitute a classificatory model of chairs. The same principle may be used to form everyday classifications of many things other than chairs. To classify items of furniture such as chairs we need to know other principles, especially those describing the changing bases of resemblance that enable the classifier to link particular chairs to the prototype.

We would suggest that formal concepts should be used to provide the predicates of polythetic categories in social science, just as they are in natural science. That is to say, one should first construct a precise mathematical model of the processes being observed and then define the predicates in terms of properties of the model, rather than of the actual collection of observed entities.

Such a construction is quite familiar to a natural scientist, but at present sociological categories tend to be directly derived from empirically discovered features of particular societies. For instance, we apply kinship terms such as *Hawaiian* or *Iroquois* and socioeconomic categories such as *hunter-gatherer* or *feudal*. However, comparative propositions about members of these kinds of categories are continually frustrated by a vast array of variations and exceptions within each of them and by inconvenient overlaps between them.

Squabbles over what the terminology really means are commonplace with this form of classification. Even when there is agreement on the data, there is no basis in these systems to resolve disagreement between two social scientists about whether a particular terminology should be extended to cover a disputed case. By adapting formal set-theoretic and graph-theoretic concepts as the predicates for grid and group, we are able to avoid fruitless disputes over the names of categories and criteria.

4.3 Defining a Social Unit

The first task in developing operational predicates for grid/group analysis is to specify the basic social unit to which the technique is to be applied. Immediately, we run into trouble with the traditional sociological terms such as *society, party, organization, sect, club, tribe, lineage,* and so forth. These terms are at once too specific and too vague for our purposes.

They are too specific in that they are tied to particular ethnocentric preconceptions about what kinds of social organizations are to be found in the world, and about how they should be studied. Although anthropologists have traditionally tended to present their material in a tribal monograph, there are really no naturally occurring categories of human social organizations that are self-evident units of analysis. The reality is that scientists cut the social pie one way or another in accordance with their own interests and inclinations, as well as with what they actually discover in their empirical research.

For purposes of grid/group analysis, we want to look at the pie in our own way. However, we also want to be able to apply our analysis to these other kinds of slices. The object is to establish a basis for comparisons and contrasts between kinds of social organization that might not be comparable according to the criteria on which they are presently studied.

For example, the sociology of religion tends to constitute its units of analysis according to the beliefs and manifest goals of churches, sects, and denominations. On the other hand, organization theory looks at the organizational dynamics of formal association, paying only superficial attention to the ideas that sustain them. This separation is as if sects and churches were not organizations with their own dynamics, and as if non-religious kinds of organization did not generate characteristic belief orientations. The outcome has impoverished our understanding of both secular and religious institutions.

At the same time as they are too specific, most established classifications of social organization are too vague for us. When is a *sect* not a sect, but rather a more loosely knit *cult,* or instead a more differentiated and hierarchical *denomination?* What criteria of ethnicity should we invoke to define a *society* or *culture?* These are areas of protracted anthropological and sociological debate that we seek to avoid in constructing a polythetic model of social organization and sustaining ideas that lends itself to grid/group analysis.

Our purpose is to show how the strength of grid- and group-type constraints can be measured across the wide range of empirical social contexts encountered by anthropologists, historians, and sociologists. Our task is to assign numbers to the strength of each polythetic coordinate. We must start with a model of social organization that fulfills two conditions. First, it must be capable of being stated mathematically, and second, it must be able to be sensitively applied by ethnographers to a variety of actual cases.

The EXACT Model

Such a model is a high level of abstraction from actual instances of social organization; it is a logical statement of the minimum conditions for social activity. In this sense, its reference is deliberately nonspecific, hence we call this a model of the basic *social unit*. It may be a sect, or a church, a regiment, a village, or a tribe. It may be even be a neighborhood bar. In the case of Lakemouth, the Chamber of Commerce, Local 387, LANE, the Scallopshell Caucus, and the dune dwellers, each can be described in the terms of this model.

All five of these social units at Lakemouth can be represented as instances of the mathematical structure called the EXACT model. The acronym EXACT facilitates recall of the five constituents of the model. There is a set X of persons who are members of the social unit, a set A of activities in which members interact, and a set C of publicly recognized roles that members adopt while participating in the activities. There is also a timespan T during which a typical distribution of activities occurs and a set E of eligible nonmembers, persons who would not be excluded from membership solely on classificatory grounds. The set E might be empty.

The set X corresponds to the established sociological concept of an interactive social network, which can be represented as a labeled graph. Two individuals x_i and x_j are linked by a line if there exists an activity a_k in which they interact. For our present purposes, we consider only social networks whose graphs are *connected*.

In measuring group, we are measuring the strength and closeness of the interactive network. We are interested in the extent to which the members interact with each other, the frequency of the interactions, and the range of activities in which they interact. We are also interested in finding out how hard it is for a new member to attach to the network.

Ethnographic Considerations

An obvious problem in using this model is how to determine the extent of the social unit, how to define its boundaries, how to determine who is inside the set X and who is outside? Social units are rarely (if ever) wholly self-contained. Some interactions take place between members and nonmembers.

The practical solution may be clearer in a high-group context than where group is low. The boundary of a high-group unit will lie where the interconnectedness of the network suddenly diminishes. This would be most clearly discernible in the case of the Scallopshell Caucus. Members of the Chamber of Commerce also interact closely with other members and their families, but less intensively with nonmembers. The point where the interconnectedness diminishes will probably be less clear in the case of Local 387, as the union members will have extensive contacts outside the unit. However, we would guess that the boundary would still be detectable in this way.

At weak group, where the network itself is loosely interconnected, it will be harder to determine the appropriate limits of the social unit chosen for study. This problem arises in looking at LANE, but is probably most obvious in the case of the dunes dwellers. This unit barely qualifies as an interactive network at all. In the first instance, it is based on common geographical location as much as on any other factor. But why not go beyond the dunes, or a factory, or outside a borough, if there is no clear boundary to the networks of those who live or work within it? Should we accept these economic or geopolitical definitions of our units of study if they are apparently irrelevant to cultural diversity?

The answer is, of course, that there is no mechanical solution to these problems. The limits of any sample are to be set in accordance with the conditions that provoked the study (Why are there poor labor relations in this factory, or why is alcoholism high in this borough?) and the interests which the ethnographer brings to bear on it.

Of course, the ethnographer must be sensitive to the members' own concept of where the boundaries of their culture lie. Where the network is loose meshed and the group boundary is unclear to the ethnographer, it seems reasonable to suppose that the individuals being studied are also aware of the ambiguous or unbounded (depending on their value orientation) character of the social group to which they belong. In contrast to the Chamber of Commerce, Local 387, or the Scallopshell Caucus, the dunes dwellers probably don't regard themselves as a community at all.

If the mesh of the social network is consistently loose, that very absence of change is a fair indication of a low-group environment. In this case the ethnographer is entitled to exercise more discretion about the size and extent of the sample than where there are clear indications that people recognize very well who is, or is not, a member of their own social unit. Unfortunately, even in communities where primary networks exist, the primary networks identified by the members themselves may not be the most appropriate units of analysis for an ethnographer interested in a particular problem. For example, in researching the effects of workplace organization on productivity, an ethnographer may be more interested in subnetworks in an office or factory than in any networks in the wider community with which the members identify themselves. When the networks the ethnographer has chosen are very sparse, such as that which connects the members of LANE, members may belong to other networks about which the ethnograhper knows little. However, the selection of sparse units, like LANE, is justified by the ethnographer's interest in the predominant collective effect that participation in LANE has on its membership.

4.4 Distinguishing Between Grid and Group Predicates

To assist the ethnographer we have identified five measurable network variables that are indicators of the comprehensiveness of a social network and the strength of its boundary. These are called *proximity, transitivity, frequency, scope,* and *impermeability*. We regard each of these measures as a basic predicate of the group dimension. Each predicate and its use in determining group strength is described in detail in the following chapters. Some of them bear close resemblance to measures already familiar to anthropologists and sociologists through network analysis. (For instance, see Freeman 1979 or White, Boorman, and Brieger 1976.) The principal novelty of group measurement, as we define it here, is that we use the justification of polythetic classification to apply several measures simultaneously.

Granovetter (1979) and Barnes (1979) have observed that until the mid-1970s, network analysis lacked theoretical richness. In particular, its models did not adequately account for the different kinds of interactions that persons might have. One attempt to remedy this was to evaluate the balance of positive (i.e., friendly or cooperative) network linkages and negative (i.e., hostile or obstructive) ones. However, its success was limited. What counts as positive or negative has to be made very specific in each case. Some linkages may be both.

In grid/group analysis, it is not necessary to evaluate the network linkages in this way. The quality of the linkages is measured independently on the separate, equally complex, grid coordinate. An established sociological precedent for our construction of grid may be found in *multiple hierarchy* analysis (Jeffries and Ransford 1980). This approach seeks to evaluate the cumulative social pressures imposed on people through their simultaneous membership in a range of separate ranked social classifications. For example, exponents of the theory argue that members of both categories *women* and *the poor* are likely to experience greater negative hierarchical constraints than their male or wealthy counterparts. By combining networks with multiple hierarchy analysis we are able to make the kinds of predictive generalizations about cosmologies and behavior that were advanced in Chapter 3, but are not possible with network analysis alone.

In measuring grid, we are concerned with differentiation within the network. Where differentiation is extensive and strongly enforced, members of the set X may not all have equal access to all of the activities in set A. For instance, in some social networks, such as the Chamber of Commerce, the classification *woman* might greatly affect a person's ascribed suitability for participation in certain activities, in which case it is a strongly enforced classification. On the other hand, another classification, say *left-handed,* might be unimportant in ascribing suitability for that same activity.

In high-grid units such as LANE, the Chamber of Commerce, or Local 387, some activities will be the exclusive preserve of members of specific office holders in a bureaucracy, of senior echelons of a hierarchy, or of members of a recognizable age-grade or caste. Even in those activities which are shared by the whole network, there may be different roles in each activity that are allocated to different categories of people. Where such roles may not be shared by the whole community, or at least may not be competed for by all, then high-grid constraints are at work. Alternatively, prototype low grid is where everyone has the right to participate in each activity and to play any role at all, or at least in turn with others. This is the case with both the Scallop-shell Caucus and the dunes dwellers.

An obvious problem in measuring grid predicates arises in distinguishing a category of persons from a social aggregation. A women's committee, or a council of elders would both seem to satisfy our criteria for a social unit, with classificatory requirements for membership, female and age, respectively. How do we sort out grid from group in such a case?

In both of these examples, the body concerned is part of a larger social whole. Unless the ethnographer is interested solely in committee structure (in which case classificatory criteria for getting on the committee in the first place will not be the object of attention so much as the division of roles and responsibilities among members once they are there) the ethnographer will have misdrawn the boundaries of the social unit. As we have seen with Local 387, the fact that committee members may meet more often and develop their own sense of being the inner wheel of a social unit will be captured by measuring their subnetwork by the same criteria as the rest of their unit. We are not seeking to measure the same thing twice. In measuring grid, we are looking at the existence of classifications constraining access to activities and roles within the social unit, not at any extra group character-istics they might induce.

Where there are classificatory conditions for group membership in the first place, as in the Chamber of Commerce, we also
have to exercise care, even though the problems are no more
insurmountable. For example, being Jewish or being black is a
classification. It is a cultural attribute of someone that affects
that person's opportunity for roles. It does not describe the extent of that person's involvement in a social aggregation, i.e., a
social network. A Jew may choose to join a synagogue or a
fraternal organization that does not admit non-Jewish members,
in which case he must satisfy a classificatory condition of membership. However, there are other Jews who are eligible and who
do not choose to join. For our purposes, the unit of analysis
would be the congregation or the organization he joins, not the
category of Jews.

By recognizing the existence of the set E of eligible nonmembers, we safeguard ourselves against confusing classificatory differentiation within a social unit, and classificatory requirements
for membership. Even where set E is empty, i.e., where all who
are eligible belong, the fact that all members of the unit share the
same classificatory requirement (e.g., being Jewish, black, female, or whatever) excludes this factor as a source of internal
differentiation.

Furthermore, we do not preclude a social unit from recognizing
and attaching importance to external status that does not depend
on the group and is not originated by it. Outside status may well
prove to be a source of internal differentiation. For instance, a
black social club might prefer to attract judges and clergymen
rather than laborers. It might admit both, but only elect professionals to its presidency. Internal differentiation need not rest on
criteria that are purely internal to the social unit, even when there
are classificatory criteria for membership. This is clearly the case
with the Chamber of Commerce at Lakemouth.

The four grid predicates we are scoring at Lakemouth are all
concerned with roles. Roles are a form of categorical distinction
that has general applicability, but there also exist other kinds of
distinction. For instance, if we have an opportunity to observe
how some fixed medium of symbolic information makes distinc-

tions, then we could measure the grid predicate called *informa-tion transmission*. This predicate has been developed in detail and tested empirically. (See Gross 1982, Gross 1983, and Douglas and Gross 1981.) In particular, we might measure the extent to which food-taking, clothing, or space allocation symbolizes categories of time, as well as of roles. Another possible grid predicate is *standardization*. One measures the extent to which behavior in certain activities is formalized or prescribed.

All that is necessary for our measurements is that status differentiation be recognized and practiced within the social unit, in the case of high grid, or be deliberately denied by it as in the case of low-grid sects. The Scallopshell Caucus exemplifies the latter case by its pointed denial of external status and internal differentiation in favor of equality among the commonwealth of believers. In order to measure these variations in the degree of internal differentiation we have identified four predicates of grid. These are: specialization, asymmetry, entitlement, and accountability. They will be explicated in the following chapters along with the group predicates already enumerated.

CHAPTER FIVE

QUANTIFYING GROUP AND GRID

We are now ready to present the EXACT model, a mathematical abstraction of a social unit. In quantitative grid/group analysis, a variant of this model is formulated early in the planning stages of an experiment. The collection of data is organized in accordance with the features of the model. The grid and group predicates are chosen by the ethnographer and defined as mathematical properties of the model, so that there is no ambiguity in calculating predicate scores from the data. From the aggregate grid and group scores, we can infer the cultural bias of the unit. This quantification of bias enables us to extend grid/group theory from a nominal description of four prototype combinations, as in section 1.3, to a continuous two-dimensional range.

5.1 The EXACT Model of a Social Unit

The EXACT model of a social unit has the following components:

X = the set of members $x_1, \ldots, x_p$ of the unit
A = the set of activities $a_1, \ldots, a_m$ in which members interact
C = the set of publicly recognized roles that members assume in the activities
T = a timespan during which a typical distribution of activities occurs
E = the set of nonmembers $e_1, \ldots, e_s$ who are eligible for admission to membership during timespan T

Thus, "EXACT" is an approximate acronym.

Although X, A, and E are sets represented as simple lists, both C and T have additional structure. In particular, the set C is partitioned into subsets $C_1, \ldots, C_m$ so that the subset C_i contains all the roles that occur in activity a_i.

The timespan T is expressed as culturally defined discrete time units, at whatever level is appropriate to the study. For instance, T might be a year whose time units are days, or a day whose units are hours or minutes. Various other structures are superimposed on T, such as weeks and months. Moreover, T includes probabilistic distributions and various algorithms that govern time-based behavior.

For instance, the principal notion of time in some cultures might be based on social reciprocity. Perhaps hospitality is reciprocated within an average of five days and a standard deviation of 1½, and perhaps roles are cycled within working units in a period whose length depends on the size of the unit. The possibilities for time structure are so many, that we deliberately avoid making confining specifications. (See Evans-Pritchard 1940, Cunnison 1951, 1957, Lévi-Strauss 1963, and Rayner 1982.)

Interactions in the social unit are expressed by the EXACT graph. For each member x_i of the unit there is a point labeled x_i. For every pair of members x_j and x_k who interact in activity a_i, there is a line labeled a_i with endpoints x_j and x_k. In a more elaborate version of the EXACT model, this line might also carry a weighting label to indicate the extent of the interaction. In any case, it is possible that there are several lines with the same two endpoints. As a social unit, one might select any collection of persons such that the EXACT graph is connected. In doubtful cases, we include the persons who interact a lot with the network and exclude the ones who do not interact.

In fact, we select social units on a basis of research interest. In this case, we are interested in units that have expressed an attitude to the proposal to build a nuclear reactor in Lakemouth, because we are interested in comparing attitudes to nuclear risks in a nearby community. If we are interested in examining trade union branches or boys clubs or whatever, we would select members of these types of organization. Of course, it is very helpful if this coincides with locally maximal group scores, and sometimes this may be the only way to define a social unit for certain types of research design.

The definitions of some of the grid and group predicates borrow some terminology from graph theory. Some standard texts of graph theory and modelling appear in the bibliography at the end of this book. The reader is forewarned that terminology varies from one text to another. Where there is a discrepancy in usage, we have sometimes opted for the general vocabulary of abstract mathematics over the special keywords of social network theory.

First of all, the *distance* $d(w_i, s_j)$ between x_i and x_j means the minimum number of lines one must traverse to get from x_i to x_j. Thus, if x_i and x_j interact in some activity, then $d(x_i, x_j) = 1$. If they do not interact with each other, but if they both interact with X_k, then $d(x_i, x_j) = 2$. A friend of a friend of a friend is at distance 3, and so on.

The *neighbor set* of a point x of a graph is defined to be the set of all points adjacent to x. Thus, in the EXACT graph, the neighbor set of a member x_i contains all members who interact with x_i. We denote this set by $N(x_i)$.

The *valence* of a point x is defined to be the number of points in the neighbor set $N(x)$.

5.2 Group Predicate Scores

We shall now give methods to compute the five group predicates that seem most applicable at Lakemouth. These are proximity, transitivity, frequency, scope, and impermeability. Other group predicates might be applied elsewhere, as one expects from our polythetic definition.

Proximity

The *proximity score* is a measure of the closeness of members to each other in the EXACT graph. It is defined so that a member

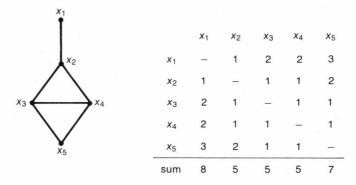

	x_1	x_2	x_3	x_4	x_5
x_1	—	1	2	2	3
x_2	1	—	1	1	2
x_3	2	1	—	1	1
x_4	2	1	1	—	1
x_5	3	2	1	1	—
sum	8	5	5	5	7

Figure 5.1. A hypothetical network and the associated table of distances

x_i who interacts with every other member of the unit in at least one activity will get a proximity score of 1, the highest possible value. If x_i interacts with only one other member, then his proximity score might be nearly 0. Obviously, many intermediate values between 0 and 1 can occur. If we assign weights to the interactions, then they might be involved in the calculation of proximity scores.

To any network, we may associate a table of distances between the points. For instance, figure 5.1 shows a network and the corresponding table. There is an easy sequence of arithmetic steps that leads from this table to the proximity score.

The entry at row x_i and column x_j is the distance between members x_i and x_j. For instance, since the minimum number of lines one must traverse to set from x_2 to x_5 is 2, the number 2 is written at row x_2 and column x_5. The bottom entry in each column is the sum of the distances in that column.

Since there are p members $x_1, \ldots , x_p$ in the social unit, and since we disregard the distance of a member from himself, the average distance from member x_j to other members is obtained as follows: divide the bottom number in column x_j by $p - 1$. In particular, since the network in figure 5.1 has 5 members, we divide each of the bottom numbers by 4, which yields the following set of average distances.

Member	x_1	x_2	x_3	x_4	x_5
Sum of distances	8	5	5	5	7
÷ 4	÷ 4	÷ 4	÷ 4	÷ 4	÷ 4
Average distances	2.0	1.25	1.25	1.25	1.75

We define *prox (x$_i$)*, the proximity score for member x_i, to be the reciprocal of his average distance to other members. Thus, for the example in figure 5.1, we compute the following individual proximity scores.

Member	x_1	x_2	x_3	x_4	x_5
Average distance	2.0	1.25	1.25	1.25	1.75
Proximity score	.50	.80	.80	.80	.57

Since members x_1 and x_5 are less centrally situated in the network than x_2, x_3 and x_4, it is to be expected that their proximity scores are lower. Our expectation is borne out by the computation.

The proximity score for the entire unit is the average of the proximity scores of the members. Thus, for the network X of figure 5.1;

$$\text{Prox } (X) = \frac{1}{5} (.50 + .80 + .80 + .57) = .694$$

Transitivity

In general mathematical usage, a relationship R is called *transitive* if whenever aRb and bRc, it follows that aRc. The prototype of a transitive relationship is $\leq$ ("less than or equal to"). Obviously, if $a \leq b$ and $b \leq c$, then $a \leq c$. Not all relationships are transitive. For instance, "is the brother-in-law of" is non-transitive, because your brother-in-law's brother-in-law is not necessarily your brother-in-law.

We are concerned with the extent to which the social interaction between members of a social unit is transitive. In other words, given that x_i interacts with x_j and that x_j interacts with x_k, what is the probability that x_i interacts with x_k? In graph-theoretic terminology, we would ask this question: Given that x_j is adjacent to x_i and to x_k, how likely is it that x_i and x_k are adjacent, in which case x_i, x_j, and x_k lie on a circuit of length 3 in the network?

In any threesome (x_i, x_j, x_k), there are three possible twosomes: (x_i, x_j), (x_i, x_k), and (x_j, x_k). The subnetwork based on the threesome (x_i, x_j, x_k) is *connected* if and only if at least two of the possible twosomes are interactive. This corresponds to the geometric observation that if there are three points in a plane and if two lines are drawn with different endpoint pairs, then the result is a connected graph. If all three of the twosomes are interactive, then the subnetwork based on (x_i, x_j, x_k) is *complete*.

If a threesome is connected but not complete, then there is an intrasitivity. We define *trans(x_i)*, the transitivity score, by the formula

$$\text{Trans } (x_i) = \frac{\text{\# complete threesomes that contain } x_i}{\text{\# connected threesomes that contain } x_i}$$

Based on this formula, we calculate the transitivity score for a member x_i in three steps. First list all the connected threesomes that contain that member. Next indicate which of the connected threesomes is complete. Then calculate trans (x_i) as a ratio. Table 5.1 shows a sample calculation for the members of the network in figure 5.1.

The unit-wide transitivity score is the average of the transitivity scores for the members. Thus, using the scores shown in table 5.1, we calculate

$$\text{Trans } (X) = \frac{1}{5} (0 + .2 + .5 + .5 + .33) = .306$$

as the score for the network in figure 5.1.

Table 5.1. Calculations of Transitivity Scores

Member	Connected Threesomes	Complete?	Transitivity Score
x_1	$x_1\, x_2\, x_3$	no	0/2 = 0
	$x_1\, x_2\, x_4$	no	
x_2	$x_1\, x_2\, x_3$	no	
	$x_1\, x_2\, x_4$	no	
	$x_2\, x_3\, x_4$	yes	1/5 = .2
	$x_2\, x_3\, x_5$	no	
	$x_2\, x_4\, x_5$	no	
x_3	$x_1\, x_2\, x_3$	no	
	$x_2\, x_3\, x_4$	yes	
	$x_2\, x_3\, x_5$	no	2/4 = .5
	$x_3\, x_4\, x_5$	yes	
x_4	$x_1\, x_2\, x_4$	no	
	$x_2\, x_3\, x_4$	yes	
	$x_2\, x_4\, x_5$	no	2/4 = .5
	$x_3\, x_4\, x_5$	yes	
x_5	$x_2\, x_3\, x_5$	no	
	$x_2\, x_4\, x_5$	no	1/3 = .33
	$x_3\, x_4\, x_5$	yes	

Frequency

The *frequency score* for a member is the proportion of his or her allocable time during which he or she interacts in some unit activity with other members of the unit. The ethnographer must decide, as explained in chapter 6, how much time each member x_i has available to allocate and how much is actually allocated to interactive unit activities. These quantities are denoted, respectively, by

$$\text{alloc-time } (x_i) \text{ and } i/a - \text{time } (x_i)$$

Then the frequency score is defined as the ratio

$$\text{Freq } (x_1) = \frac{i/a - \text{time } (x_i)}{\text{alloc-time } (x_i)}$$

The unit-wide frequency score is the average of the member

frequency scores. Thus, a high score means that members spend nearly all their available time with other members.

Scope

If a given social unit is a subnetwork of some larger system, or if its membership overlaps with the membership of other networks, then a person's commitment might extend beyond the given unit. The *scope score* measures a person's diversity of interactive involvement in the activities of a given unit, relative to his interactive involvement outside the unit.

For each member x_i, we define unit i/a number (x_i) to be the number of activities of the unit in which x_i interacts with other members. We also define

total i/a number (x_i)

to be the number of activities both inside and outside the unit, in which x_i interacts with other persons. Then

$$\text{Scope } (x_i) = \frac{\text{unit } i/a \text{ number } (x_i)}{\text{total } i/a \text{ number } (x_i)}$$

Thus, scope $(x_i) = 1$ means that member x_i does not engage in any activity with non-members that does not also include other members, while scope (x_i) near zero means that x_i interacts primarily with nonmembers. The unit-wide scope score is the average of the member scores.

Impermeability

The *impermeability score* measures the likelihood that a non-member who satisfies the categorical requirements for membership and wants to join will actually attain membership. Unlike the four other group predicates defined here, impermeability is defined only on a unit-wide basis.

The entry ratio of a unit is the proportion of eligible nonmembers who want to join that actually does join the unit during a typical timespan. We define the impermeability score of the unit by

$$\text{Imperm } (X) = 1 - \text{entry ratio } (X)$$

Hence, an impermeability score near one means that the unit is nearly impossible to enter. At the opposite extreme, a score of zero means that all eligibles are admitted.

Variations

The five group predicates applied to Lakemouth are not necessarily the best selection for other situations. In some situations, it might be appropriate to weight heavily certain kinds of experience in calculating *scope,* for example. Some particular subset of special activities might be the basis for what members perceive as a *commonality of experience,* and they should receive additional weight. Other activities might involve *life-support dependence,* and they should be weighted accordingly.

Identifying activities and weighting their importance is a decision of ethnography, not of mathematics. The ethnographer is also responsible for selecting and justifying the predicates.

5.3 Grid Predicate Scores

Four grid predicates will be applied to the Lakemouth dispute. This section describes how to calculate scores for *specialization, asymmetry, entitlement,* and *accountability.* As in the case of group predicates, an ethnographer might select a different set under other circumnstances.

Specialization

The word *specialization* is used here in the sense of narrowness, not of expertise within a domain. It is the opposite of diversification. We are interested in the proportion of the possible roles that a member x_i actually assumes during a typical time-span. (Some problems of defining roles are discussed in section 6.1). Let # roles (C) denote the total number of roles available within the unit and # roles (x_i) the number of roles assumed by x_i.

We define the *specialization score* for x_i by the equation

$$\text{Spec } (x_i) = 1 - \frac{\text{\# roles } (x_i)}{\text{\# roles } (C)}$$

If some roles seem more important than others, then the formula on the right-hand side could be adjusted to reflect weighting of roles. The unit-wide specialization score is defined to be the average of the member scores.

Asymmetry

The predicate called *asymmetry* is a measure of the lack of symmetry in role exchanges among members. For instance, if someone returns someone else's hospitality, that is an instance of symmetry in the roles of host and guest. Some role pairs, such as servant and master, are unlikely to be exchanged. A high asymmetry score means that roles are usually not exchanged.

Our starting point in calculating a member's asymmetry score is to consider his relationship to one other member. Suppose that x_i and x_j are any two members, and let c_u and c_v be a pair of roles such that there is an interaction in which x_i occupies c_u while x_j occupies c_v. The role pair (c_u, c_v) is called a *one-way* pair for x_i and x_j if x_i and x_j do not exchange them during the time-span.

We define the *pairwise asymmetry score* asym (x_i, x_j) to be the ratio of the number of one-way role pairs for x_i and x_j to the total number of role pairs. Of course, this score is undefined if x_i and x_j do not interact. In a more elaborate analysis, one might weight the importance of roles or the time spent in them or the number of distinct interactions as factors in the definition of asym (x_i, x_j).

The necessity for doing so is to be determined by the ethnographer.

The asymmetry score for a member x_i is simply the average of his pairwise asymmetry scores, taken over the set of members with whom x_i interacts. It is immediately clear from the definition of the EXACT graph that the number of members with whom x_i interacts is valence (x_i). Thus, the asymmetry score for x_i equals

$$\frac{1}{\text{valence } (x_i)} \Sigma \text{ asym } (x_i, x_j)$$

Thus, an asymmetry score of zero for x_i corresponds to complete symmetry, while an asymmetry score of one indicates the total absence of role exchanges. The unit-wide asymmetry score is defined to be the average of the asymmetry scores for the individual members.

Entitlement

The next predicate is based on a familiar distinction in anthropology. Some roles are attained by *achievement;* that is, they are open to competition. Other roles are attained by *ascription,* so that access to them is limited to certain restrictive categories of person. We define the *entitlement score* for a member to be the proportion of ascribed roles to all roles. That is,

$$\text{Entitlement } (x_i) = \frac{\#\text{ ascribed roles } (x_i)}{\#\text{ roles } (x_i)}$$

The entitlement score for the unit is the average over the membership.

Accountability

The fourth and last predicate we consider is *accountability,* by which we mean immediate accountability. Suppose that members

x_i and x_j interact in the roles c_u and c_v. Suppose also that one of these roles, but not both, includes sanctions that are used in exacting performance from the occupant of the other role. Then these respective roles are called the *dominant role* and the *subordinate role*. In determining dominant and subordinate roles, we take into account both coercive sanctions, such as fines and suspension from membership, and noncoercive sanctions, such as incurring disapproval or the application of moral pressure.

The *set of accountability interactions* of members x_i and x_j is defined to be the subset of role interactions between x_i and x_j such that one of the roles is dominant and the other subordinate, and it is denoted

acc/roles (x_i, x_j)

The *accountability score* for x_i is the proportion of his role interactions in which he is either dominant or subordinate. Precisely, we define

$$\text{Acc } (x_i) = \frac{\Sigma_j \ \# \ \text{acc/roles } (x_i, x_j)}{\Sigma_j \ \# \ \text{roles } (x_i, x_j)}$$

This formal definition is consistent with our viewpoint that member x_i is likely to have his sensitivity to categorical distinctions strengthened either when he accounts to someone else or when someone else is accountable to him. The accountability score for a unit is the average over the membership.

5.4 Aggregating Predicates

Once the predicate scores are obtained, the remaining step is to aggregate them into composite scores for grid and group. If the predicates are of equal importance and structurally independent, then the obvious way to compose them is to take an average. For instance, one could add five group predicate scores and divide by five or add four grid predicate scores and divide by four.

If some predicates seem more important than others, then they may be weighted accordingly in the averaging process. What this means is that each score is first multiplied by a weight to obtain a weighted score. Next the weighted scores are added. Then the sum of the weighted scores is divided by the sum of the weights. The quotient is called a *weighted average*.

For instance, suppose there was an ethnographically sound reason to consider specialization and accountability twice as important as asymmetry and to consider entitlement three times as important. Then we would calculate the grid score as

$$\frac{1}{8}\{2 \cdot \text{spec}(x) + 2 \cdot \text{acc}(x) + 1 \cdot \text{asym}(x) + 3 \cdot \text{entitlement}(x)\}$$

Of course, the usual average is just a special case of the weighted average in which all weights are the same, usually the number 1. Needless to say, the weights must not be assigned at liberty, otherwise any desired result can be obtained. Weights should be established during the design phase, and justified in accordance with the anticipated empirical features of the research.

The resulting values for grid score and group score are numbers between zero and one. Together these scores may be represented as a single point on a one-by-one diagram, called the *continuous grid/group diagram*. However, it should be understood that both grid and group are ordinal scales with a metric, not interval scales.

Scales

On a simple ordinal scale, it could be said only that one unit outranks another, or that it is much higher in the ranking. Our metric permits us to say whether one unit has much more or just slightly more of the measured characteristic, regardless of the number of units being ranked.

By way of contrast, an interval scale would permit us to say that a difference of .4 is four times as great as a difference of .1.

We can do this for height and weight, but not for grid or group. Furthermore, on an interval scale, measured values in two different settings are comparable. With grid and group, the burden of establishing comparability rests on the ethnographer.

5.5 How Different Are the Predicates?

There are superficial reasons why two of our predicate scores might appear to be measuring the same thing. However, whatever correlations are discovered empirically are aspects of culture and organization, not of our mathematical model.

As an example, we shall now consider the group predicates proximity and transitivity. A complete graph has scores of 1.0 in both predicates, while a long chain has transitivity 0.0 and proximity near zero. Thus, they can be simultaneously high or simultaneously low. However, the existence of these extreme examples of correlation are only a small part of the range of possibilities.

In theory, it would be possible to mix high proximity with low transitivity, as illustrated in figure 5.2. Every point of the network shown has proximity score .70. The transitivity score is zero, because there are no circuits of length three.

It is also theoretically possible to have low proximity and high transitivity, as illustrated in concept by figure 5.3. The idea is that complete graphs are assembled into a chain with connecting rods.

The graph in figure 5.3 has two kinds of vertices—the ones at the ends of connecting rods, and all the others. If the big cliques

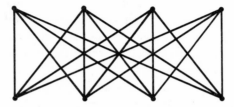

Figure 5.2. A network with high proximity and low transitivity

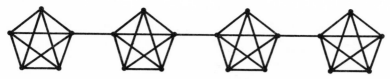

Figure 5.3. How to obtain low proximity and high transitivity simultaneously

are complete graphs of m vertices, then vertices at the end of connecting rods will have transitivity scores of $(m-2)/(m+2)$, while others have transitivity scores near to 1.0. With big cliques (i.e., many more vertices than the five shown in figure 5.3), the transitivity score of the rod ends approaches 1.0, and the ratio of rod-ends to other vertices will be small. Thus the transitivity score of the entire network will be close to one.

On the other hand, if the chain is very long, the proximity score will be low. In fact, it may be arbitrarily close to zero. Thus, we can obtain very high transitivity and very low proximity simultaneously.

Whether networks like the ones shown in figures 5.2 and 5.3 are likely to occur in real cases is, of course, an empirical question. What they do establish is that the mathematical structure of the EXACT model permits mixtures of scores. Since these two predicates are the most difficult pair to distinguish, among all that we have described, we will not discuss other possible dependencies besides proximity and transitivity.

As experience with quantitative grid/group analysis accumulates, it may transpire that regular empirical dependencies do exist either among the basic predicates of grid or among those of group. If this does turn out to be the case, it might be possible to rely on measurements of a smaller number of predicates from which to construct composite grid/group scores. However, we would emphasise that, in such cases, the dependencies would be empirical correlations that can only be discovered by application of the model to concrete cases. They should not be features of the model. In conceiving a new predicate, one should consider whether it is structurally tied to the others, and avoid any that merely reproduces a measurement that can already be made by an existing predicate.

CHAPTER SIX

AN OPERATIONAL GUIDE

This final chapter serves as an operational guide to the execution of a grid/group experiment. Our intent is illustrated by a description of the details of the analysis at Lakemouth.

A quantitative grid/group analysis is performed in a sequence of steps. An initial hurdle is to become thoroughly acquainted with the qualitative aspects of the setting. The social units, their respective programs of activities, the roles of members, and the cultural timespan must be correctly identified in order to collect data for scoring purposes.

We describe the methods of observation, the principles of experimental design, and the techniques of recording data that are appropriate to our paradigm. It is possible to modify them to meet the special needs of a study. However, an analyst who adopts variations on them assumes the burden of proving that the variations introduce insignificant error, whether they are introduced for reasons of principle, or of economy and convenience.

6.1 Methods of Observation and Data Collection

An inept or careless attempt at grid/group analysis has no more chance of success than a comparable approach in a chemistry laboratory. Given that an experiment is not physically hazardous, a chemist usually gets a chance to repeat an experiment that is bungled on the first try. Indeed, the possibility of replicating experiments in every detail is often considered to be one of the distinguishing features of natural science. In many sociological experiments, however, there is only one chance to make correct observations, since the phenomena of interest can vary with time.

Participant Observation

Participant observation is a distinctive tool of anthropologists, and it is the ideal method to be used in a grid/group study. Although participant observation has been traditionally applied to small-scale societies, it is now increasingly the method of choice in studies of our own society that seek deep understanding of a social phenomenon.

The Professional Stranger, by Michael Agar (1980), is an invaluable guide to the theory and practice of participant observation which fairly assesses its merits and pitfalls. Briefly, the technique requires ethnographers to live among the people they are studying, to share their experience to the fullest extent permitted by the circumstances, and faithfully to record the way of life and beliefs of the people, while scrupulously guarding against personal bias.

The participant observer is usually required to avoid changing the course of events. This is partly an ethical consideration (which may or may not be misguided) and partly a practical one. So far as possible, the ethnographer wants to know what the people among whom he is living would do were he not there. Perhaps ironically, this unobtrusive profile is probably most difficult to maintain in the study of traditional societies, where participant observation has been most used. Of course, a stranger's presence inevitably changes the circumstances to some extent, but probably to a far lesser degree than sending in a team of market-research interviewers brandishing clipboards.

Questionnaires

Participant observation does not rule out the partial use of questionnaires. Indeed, to many quantitative sociologists, a detailed questionnaire aimed at the citizens of Lakemouth would be an obvious way of collecting the data we need to calculate grid/group scores.

Perhaps we could ask people to list their principal foci of social activity, such as the clubs, churches, political parties and fraternal organizations to which they belong. Similarly, we could ask them to list all the other members with whom they interact during a given week. Using a computer we could work out the proximity scores of each respondent in relation to every other member of his social network.

Transitivity could conceivably be scored by computing the connectedness of the networks. By asking people to count the number of hours a week they spend with each of the persons that they list, we could arrive at frequency scores. Scope might be simple enough to elicit from a questionnaire by asking respondents to list everything they do, and put code marks by those activities that are specific to any of the social organizations with which they identify. Permeability might be harder to measure by questionnaire, but we could ask people how much time elapsed between their electing to join an organization and their acceptance in it, or whether on any given date they were trying to obtain membership to any particular body for which they were eligible.

Unfortunately there are serious drawbacks to gathering group data by questionnaire alone. Questionnaires rely on all respondents interpreting the questions in the same way; in particular, questionnaires require respondents to decide what is important to the investigator and what can be left out. When asked to list social activities, respondent X might include his every interaction with someone else, while respondent Y might list only those he considers important or interesting, and omit many of the activities which appear in X's list. Since we are in the business of finding out which activities are significant group factors in order to be able to count them, we are not in a position, at this stage, to specify what constitutes a significant interaction in either case. We simply cannot advise questionnaire respondents in advance whether or not greeting someone they pass in the street is an interaction we wish to measure.

A questionnaire would, therefore, gather much more data than is strictly necessary to measure group scores. We would have to collect lists of names and of interactions, not just numbers, because we cannot rely on different respondents to count the same things. These cumbersome lists would then have to be inspected and edited before counting could begin.

Unless the editor is already very familiar with the social context of each of the respondents, this process might introduce further subjective inaccuracies into the measurements. Furthermore, the huge quantity of data gathered in relation to that actually used might engender inflated impressions of accuracy.

Similar problems arise in designing grid questionnaires. In measuring specialization, asymmetry, entitlement, or accountability, questionnaires leave too much room for the individual interpretations of respondents. If simply asked to list the number of roles taken on during a week, and the number of times each one is adopted, a respondent, rather than the ethnographer, has to decide which actions are role-specific. If X, rather than X's spouse, winds the alarm clock because it is on X's side of the bed, it would be absurd to suggest that X bears the role of alarm clock winder. But, to what extent can we rely on members of the lay public to decide where absurdity ends and meticulous recording of roles begins? It is hard enough to achieve consensus on such matters among trained social scientists, but it is they, not their subjects, who must decide what counts as a role for the purposes of grid/group analysis.

The problems with the use of questionnaires for the kind of research we propose are not new. They may not prove insurmountable by experienced questionnaire designers with sufficient patience and ingenuity, as well as some firsthand knowledge of the field. Of course, participant observers can, and should where possible, use questionnaires to elicit some kinds of data. For example, asking people to fill in time sheets may be the best way of discovering how people use their allocable time when the observer cannot be with them constantly on a daily basis. Questionnaires are particularly suitable for obtaining details of people's cosmologies. However, this aspect of grid/group theory itself throws up an objection to our using questionnaire data which may not easily be overcome.

It is a fundamental proposition of grid/group theory that people interpret the world differently according to the social pressures of the particular grid/group quadrant they occupy. A questionnaire might be an appropriate tool for eliciting their cosmology, but it is an inescapable fact that respondents' answers to questions about their social organization will be subject to that same cosmological bias. If we are to avoid banal circularity, the data required for grid/group measurement must be obtained by careful participant observation, rather than by asking people to describe their activities through a questionnaire.

For large social units we would be happy to think that questionnaires could be designed to test whether a sample measured by observation is representative. But, for strict accuracy, our first resort for scoring each of the grid/group predicates would be participant observation. In short, before conducting an experiment, there is a critical preliminary step of gaining familiarity with the situation to be studied. At the very least, it is necessary to identify the different social units and their calendars of activities.

The next task is to design code sheets that encompass all the *initial conditions* of the EXACT models, that is, the conditions at time zero of the timespan. If the observer is already well acquainted with a social unit, then perhaps most of these data are already known. The rest are to be observed on site.

For each social unit, there is a separate model, for which one must list the names of all persons who are members at the start of the timespan during which measurement is made, and also the names of all persons who are eligible to join the unit during that timespan. For each activity in each social unit, all roles must be listed. Moreover, each role must be classified either as achieved or as ascribed.

The initial conditions do not provide enough information even to draw the EXACT graph, much less to calculate the predicate scores. Numerous *dynamic details,* which pertain to social interactions observed during the prescribed timespan, must also be recorded. Ideally, one would record every distinct interaction. However, for practical purposes, one only needs to collect a sufficiently large sample to infer predicate scores within tolerable error limits. Only for very small social units can sampling be avoided. Ove Frank (1979) discusses some of the problems that arise in sampling large social networks.

For each occurrence of each activity of each social unit, an observer records the amount of time that each member participates. Moreover, for each interaction of each member of that unit, an observer records the name of the other party to the interaction and the roles adopted by both parties. The analysis is developed entirely in terms of dyadic interactions, and therefore, the dyads must be clearly identified. (It is quite conceivable that an EXACT model could be enriched by consideration of triadic and other higher-order interactions that are mathematically modeled by hypergraphs. See R. H. Atkin 1974 and S. Seidman 1981 for instance.) It must be specified whether the interaction is an accountability interaction, in which case the dominant and subordinate roles must be distinguished. For each member, an observer must also record that person's amount of allocable time and number of external interactive activities. Some suitable form of estimation may be employed.

6.2 The Research Experience at Lakemouth

The dispute at Lakemouth attracted widespread attention from the press, even in its early stages. A team of sociologists, anthropologists and political scientists collectively engaged in public-policy analysis at a northeastern university happened to read newspaper reports identifying the diverse parties with a stake in the outcome.

Lakemouth seemed to them to be an ideal location for a cultural analysis of public attitudes toward nuclear power. The desirability of such a study had already been perceived by the research team. They felt that there were gaps in the existing information on the subject, which had been gathered by public opinion pollsters and survey analysts, and they saw an opportunity to make a deeper study with grid/group analysis.

The research team began by writing letters to the four voluntary organizations concerned: the Chamber of Commerce, Local 387, LANE, and the Scallopshell Caucus. The letters asked whether two representatives could visit each organization in Lakemouth, to discuss the possibilities of carrying out their policy analysis research program. At this point, the researchers were unsure how to approach the dunes dwellers, so they sent a talented graduate student on a preliminary visit to Lakemouth, charged with the task of finding a suitable way into that community.

The Chamber of Commerce eagerly accepted the team's proposal. Their reply hinted that they hoped that such an investigation by members of a reputable university would expose the irrationality of their opponents in the dispute. In truth, however, some members informed of the request were not so keen on the idea, fearing that trendy sociologists might have a detached liberal bias in favor of the antinuclear campaign.

LANE also responded encouragingly. Its leaders felt that cooperation with the research project would reflect well on their image as responsible and concerned citizens.

Local 387 did not express an attitude in its reply, which had been fully discussed by its executive committee. However, the union secretary did write that members of the executive committee would be willing to receive the research team's representatives to discuss the proposal.

The Scallopshell Caucus was totally noncommittal. It would make no special arrangements to meet the research team, because it did not see that this exercise would do much to stem the tide of nuclear power. Neither would it delegate the task of meeting the team to officers of the caucus, for it had none. However, the Scallops were prepared to allow two members of the research team to explain their request to a meeting of the entire caucus, should such a meeting coincide with their visit. In fact, the caucus was quite evenly divided between those who rejected collaboration as a diversion from their struggle and those who favored cooperation because of the publicity it might bring to the organization.

As it happened, the representatives of the research team were able to meet with all of the four organizations during a four-day visit to the town, at which time they persuaded each one to accept the presence of a participant observer. The graduate student member also discovered an *entrée* into the dunes community. Inquiries in the town revealed that the day-to-day maintenance of all the properties on the dunes was the responsibility of the local real estate company that participated in the development of the houses.

In fact, this arrangement had been designed to obviate any need for the homeowners to make collective decisions about the upkeep of roads, beaches, and open spaces on the dunes. It also served to maintain the privacy of homeowners and their guests by controlling access to the site at a permanently staffed gatehouse. The owner of the real estate company (a rival of Jack Loveland) saw no objection to taking on a member of the research team as gatekeeper and administrative assistant in the estate office during the summer while various members of his regular staff took their vacations.

A team of five ethnographers, three women and two men, was duly assembled and dispatched to Lakemouth for three months during the summer. The NRC licensing hearing was in full swing during this time and all of the groups were actively engaged in campaigning. It was also a time of extensive social activity in Lakemouth. The Chamber of Commerce was organizing its Fourth of July celebration, in addition to a busy round of barbecues and cocktail parties. Local 387 held a barn dance and several picnics for members' family and friends, and near the end of the period of participant observation they were preparing for Labor Day celebrations.

LANE members did not engage in much collective social activity, but some supporters strengthened preexisting friendships at various private parties and summer outings. The Scallopshell Caucus was busy with its Alternative Energy Festival, and, of course, the summer weather brought the dunes dwellers to their vacation homes more frequently than would be expected during the winter months.

The members of the ethnographic team were attached to one

or another of these organizations for the entire three-month period. We now describe their experiences as participant observers.

The Chamber of Commerce

The Chamber of Commerce permitted a female researcher not only to observe all of its meetings and social functions, but also to interview its members. She was also invited to members' homes for private gatherings and informal occasions. Records of proceedings and most of the Chamber's documents were made available upon request. The exceptions were chiefly confidential records concerned with the business dealings of individual members.

There was no room for the researcher to actually participate in the running of the Chamber of Commerce, since, as outsiders, no member of the research team would have been eligible for membership. The C of C has no employees or permanent office staff of its own. Typing and other administrative functions are carried out in the business offices of its members, so this sort of employment was also precluded. As a woman, the observer received special courtesies and suffered no disadvantage at the hands of male chamber members. She probably secured better access than a man would have, to both the family life and the women's activities associated with the chamber.

Local 387

A male researcher was permitted to assist at the business offices of Local 387 as an unpaid administrative assistant, where he helped out with running errands and preparing publicity materials. A paid position would be available only to a *bona fide* union member. He was permitted to attend all of the union's business meetings and, after a while, he was even entrusted with the task of taking minutes at some of the committee meetings.

The researcher's genuine interest in the affairs of the union soon won him popularity with its members, and he was found lodgings with the family of one of its officers. His administrative duties did not take up too much of the day and he had ample time to conduct interviews with members and their families outside of the union hall. Before the end of his stay in Lakemouth, he was even asked to give a talk on political science at one of the union's educational evenings.

LANE

LANE proved particularly straightforward to work with. A male researcher took a seasonal job in a local camera supply and hobby shop owned by a LANE member. He was easily accepted as a LANE supporter, particularly when he offered some expertise in the production of posters and handbills. Any problems encountered by this researcher had little to do with suspicion or antagonism on the part of other members. The chief difficulty was trying to record the life-styles of the individual members, as these are more diverse and less interconnected than in the other organizations.

The Scallopshell Caucus

Another female researcher was assigned to the Scallopshell Caucus. She boarded at the home of an activist and was accepted as a member of the caucus periphery, but did not take the oath. Not surprisingly, members of the caucus treated her with some reservations throughout her stay, partly because they feared that she would communicate some of their plans for nonviolent direct action to other members of the research team who might pass them on to the Chamber of Commerce or to Local 387.

The researcher's commitment to the antinuclear cause was also questioned by some members of the caucus, who objected to the idea that the research program claimed neutrality on the power station issue. Although they liked the researcher personally, they felt that the caucus should not cooperate with a research program unless it was committed to their aims. Their members finally agreed to accept the researcher because of an overall consensus in the organization that the study might provide useful publicity for its cause. However, the researcher was still excluded from certain events and information that made her task one of the most difficult in the program.

The Dunes Dwellers

The last member of the research team took up the appointment, offered by the real estate company, as gatekeeper and administrative assistant at the dunes office. From this position she was able to observe the comings and goings of the dunes dwellers firsthand. She was also given access to the records of how long each family had owned property there. She talked freely with other company officials about the habits of the dunes dwellers, and even got to know some of the most regular weekend visitors. At the end of her stay she was permitted to interview any of the homeowners who were willing to spare the time. Two-thirds of the families were interviewed in this way and were happy to cooperate with someone they had already come to know in connection with her work for the real estate company.

To meet their ethical obligations to the people they studied (Agar 1980), the research team was careful to ensure that their presence and goals were known. Everyone in Lakemouth with whom the research team had contact was made aware of their identities as ethnographers and of their purpose in studying the controversy over the nuclear plant.

The Scallopshell Caucus agreed at a meeting of all its members to participate in the study. The officers of LANE, of Local 387, and of the Chamber of Commerce each consulted its membership, and subsequently presented the research team with letters of consent. The real estate agent in charge of the dunes sent to each homeowner there a letter explaining his intention to cooperate with the project, provided that none of the owners objected, which none did. The researchers and their funding agency were satisfied that the requirements of informed consent had been fulfilled.

6.3 **Ethnographies and Predicate Scores of the Five Units**

This section presents a high-level summary of the EXACT ethnographies of each of the five social units identified in the Lakemouth dispute and an additional level of detail for the Chamber of Commerce. The same principles of descriptive method apply to each of the other four units, even though each unit has its own special features. The various predicate scores and the composite scores for grid and group are calculated.

Names of members and details of the roles and interactions are omitted, of course, since it is pointless to give them for a fictitious example. To protect the privacy of individuals, it is likely that even in a real ethnography, many such details would be presented only in the forms of statistical summaries and general qualitative characterizations.

Chamber of Commerce

The three-month fieldwork period was sufficiently long to permit observation of every activity of the Chamber of Commerce. However, estimates of the number of activities outside the unit and estimates of the time spent on such activities are rather rough. The scoring of scope and frequency requires such data, but limitations on time and access to homes of members diminished the possible accuracy. Subdividing the time-span into hourly chunks introduced a minor amount of round-off error. Restriction to a small sample of weeks and months was undoubtedly a more serious source of error.

The Chamber often seems more interested in the social lives of its fifteen members and their families than in improving the sorry state of commerce. The following list shows the eight principal kinds of activities that the Chamber of Commerce observer identified during her summer in Lakemouth:

Monthly meeting of all members
Meetings of standing committees
Community-wide social events sponsored by the chamber
Organizational meetings for chamber social events

Private gatherings with many chamberites attending
Sunday morning church service
Meetings of the Republican Club
Golf

Not all of the members of the chamber belong to the same church, and not all attend as regularly as others. However, most chamber members share an image of themselves as models of propriety. "I missed you in church," is what one member might say to another, as a way of soliciting an explanation for an absence. Although not all chamber members are Republicans, the general sentiment is that the Republican Party is the party of business. Several of the members do not play golf, and the golfers do not restrict themselves entirely to matches with other members.

Defining the activities that were to be specifically identified with the chamber was scarcely an easy matter. For instance, most of the members were somehow involved with the Little League baseball activity for children. However, the observer detected that this involvement was expected by the community from all business owners and parents of children aged 9 to 12, not just from chamber members. Accordingly, it is not listed as a chamber activity.

On the other hand, the observer had a good reason to include participation in Republican Party affairs. By cross-checking past records of chamber membership and Republican Party activities, she learned that an eligible nonmembers' chance of election to membership was correlated to an increase in party activity in the year or two immediately preceding election to chamber membership. Moreover, active Republican Party members were more likely to have their chamber memberships extended.

None of the members that the observer interviewed admitted that any specific nonbusiness activity influenced the elections to membership. Some said that interest in community life was important. However, it apparently helped to be interested in some aspects of community life and did not help to be interested in others.

Nine of the fifteen members interacted with every other mem-

Figure 6.1. The dyadic relationships that do not occur (i.e., the edge–complement) of the EXACT graph for the Chamber of Commerce

ber during the period of observation. There were two others who did not interact with each other, but did interact with all the others. Even the least active member had some dealing with all but three other members. Thus, of all the possible adjacencies in the EXACT graph (for 15 people, there are 105 possible dyads), all but four were realized, as illustrated in figure 6.1.

In order to construct the EXACT graph, the investigator compiled attendance records for every one of the activities listed earlier. The C of C itself maintained attendance records for its formal meetings. The number of members of the chamber is sufficiently small that it seemed reasonable to presume that there was an interaction between any two who attended the same meeting. Actually greeting each other or otherwise making explicit contact is not the only possible kind of interaction to be considered.

One might have expected every pair of members to interact, in view of such a liberal definition of interaction for the chamber and of such a small membership. However, some persons kept on missing each other. In assemblies of larger numbers of persons, such as at church, simultaneous attendance was not considered an interaction. From the EXACT graph for the chamber, we can compute the proximity and transitivity scores as .97 and .90, respectively to two decimal places.

Readers may wonder why we give two digits when most likely measurement is significant to only one digit. This is based on a general principle of measurement that retains the first insignificant digit. Suppose we had two measurements, .24 and .16. Since the difference in readings, of .08, is closer to .1 than to 0, we would say that the first figure indicates more of the property being measured than the second (though probably not .08 more). If the difference in the readings, to the first insignificant digit, is less than .05 we would say that the measurements indicate equal quantities of the property. Had we rounded both measurements to .2, we would have made the mistake of calling them equal.

A frequency score of .52 indicates that members spend about half of their allocable time in the listed activities. To make this measurement, the ethnographer asked each member of the chamber to keep an hour-by-hour log for one week. She also arranged to accompany a few of the members for both a working day and a weekend day.

In a formal sense, there was little discrepancy between self-reported data and observed data. However, some of the members scarcely seemed to work at all during working hours. They read their alumni magazines in the back offices, chatted with business acquaintances, and created a social ambiance for their favorite customers. Of course, others worked very hard. The ethnographer wished that it had been possible to distinguish merely being present from working. Unfortunately, there was no opportunity for her to do so on a systematic basis. She regarded the lack of discrimination as a substantive source of error in the tabulation of allocable time, which propagated into the frequency scores.

Even though other interactive activities, such as Little League, were available, most members had too little time to be involved with many of them. The scope score for the Chamber of Commerce was .72.

During the summer of observation, there appeared to be about 20 nonmembers who would be eligible at the next regular election in January. Three of them were elected at that time to replace members whose terms were over, but two nonpermanent members were reelected. Therefore, the impermeability score was .85. These predicate scores yield an aggregate group score of .79.

The observer listed a total of 29 roles, of which the average member occupied slightly more than three. Aside from host-guest interactions, roles were never exchanged. For the most part, the occupancy of roles reflected the community social hierarchy, as seen by the permanent members. Therefore, the ethnographer counted them as ascribed roles within the chamber, irrespective of whether the external status, on which the chamber role was based, might have been achieved. For example, if it had been the case that the president of the bank always filled the office of president of the Chamber of Commerce, the latter role would count as ascribed, no matter how competitively any individual may have achieved the office of bank president.

Financial success did not win Jack Loveland an invitation to membership, and he had once angrily characterized the chamber as a "middle-aged high-school clique." Permanent members seemed to have acquired a repertoire of subtle nods and gestures to indicate approval or disapproval of the short-term members, but this patronization hardly affected the behavior of the short-term members.

The grid predicate scores were as follows: specialization, .90; asymmetry, .88; entitlement, .97; and accountability, .23. Thus, the composite grid score was .75.

Local 387

Local 387 had 220 members at the beginning of the summer the observer was present. Several retired, two moved out of town, and one quit, in order to start his own small business. Of 19 applicants for membership, all recent graduates of the local high school, 17 were inducted. When jobs became scarce, the members became reluctant to admit anyone who had not grown up in Lakemouth. In practice, this hardly mattered, since rarely did anyone move to Lakemouth to find a job.

The union organizes a range of activities that varies with the season. Those that were observed during the summer are listed below. Even though the union has no explicit interest in church attendance, and despite the fact that no more than 35 percent of the members belong to any one church, its inclusion seemed appropriate, because the central members of the union network are all churchgoers. Their private discussions before and after the services are often concerned with union affairs. Activities of Local 387 were:

General meetings of all members
Meetings of the executive committee
Meetings of the standing committees
Educational evenings
Wednesday evening film series
Picnics
Barn dances
Labor Day carnival
Bowling league
Organizing committees for social events
Church attendance

As might be expected of a large network, not all of the members interact with each other. However, four was the maximum distance between any two members, and few pairs were that far apart. The unit-wide proximity score was .48. Due to clustering in subnetworks, the transitivity score for Local 387 was .88.

Union members spent proportionately more of their allocable time with their families than did the members of the Chamber of Commerce, so that their frequency score was .37, somewhat lower than the chamber. Those union members who were interviewed all reported that during contract negotiations or strikes, they would have spent most of their time with other union members, whether on union business or just to give each other support during unsettled times.

On the other hand, what time the union members allocated to non-union activities was not for interactions in the domains of other social networks. Thus, the scope score was .94, considerably higher than for the Chamber of Commerce. From the entry ratio for eligible nonmembers, we calculate an impermeability score of .11. The average of these five group predicate scores is .56, which is therefore the composite group score for the unit.

The union members were highly specialized in their union activities, just as in their work, and they rarely exchanged roles. The specialization and asymmetry scores were .92 and .89, respectively. Committee chairmen and activity organizers behaved almost like foremen, telling everyone what to do and griping about performance. The accountability score was .95. By way of contrast, the entitlement score was only .26, since relatively few roles were attained by ascription. These four grid predicate scores yield a composite grid score of .76, which is nearly the same as for the Chamber of Commerce, even though the two units differ greatly in accountability and entitlement.

Dunes Dwellers

There was only one interactive activity to be found among the dunes dwellers—an occasional cocktail hour. Sometimes it was followed by a makeshift dinner, such as pizza or take-out Chinese food from a second-floor diner over a nearby gas station. Such hospitality was usually reciprocated within a few days.

One family interacted with nearly all of the others during the period of observation, but few of the possible interaction pairs were realized, as indicated by the EXACT graph in figure 6.2. A unique feature of the data for the dunes dwellers is that their interactions are reckoned on a household basis. It would often have been impossible to schedule immediate returns of invitations if it were necessary for both principal members of the guest and host households to be present.

From the EXACT graph, the unit-wide proximity and transitivity scores are calculated to be .56 and .16, respectively. Since each household is primarily an activity center unto itself, with its own transient guest population, both the frequency score and the scope score are low, .07 and .20, respectively. The notion of

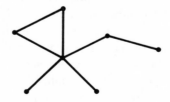

Figure 6.2. EXACT graph for the dunes households

eligible members is inapplicable here, so the group score of .25 is obtained by averaging only the four applicable group predicates. This was the only social unit among the five in which it was not possible to calculate all five group predicate scores.

There are only two roles in the dunes, host and guest, both of which are occupied by everyone. Thus, the specialization score is 0. The asymmetry score is .14, because there was one instance of an unreciprocated invitation. The entitlement score is 0, because neither of the roles is ascribed. The accountability score is 0, because the interactions do not involve sanctions. The composite grid score for the dunes is .035.

LANE

From observing LANE activities, one gets the impression of a collection of ten to twelve clusters of persons, organized according to external criteria such as neighborhood or employment. Six activities for LANE are listed below, all but one of which is business precipitated by the controversy over the reactor. Deciding to include private parties as an activity of LANE was based on the fact that LANE members typically informed the observer that they were not ordinarily party-going persons and that the topics of conversation at their parties were usually related to the reactor. Activities of LANE were:

General meetings
Litigation committee
Lobbying committee
Publicity committee
NRC licensing hearings
Private parties

Some of the forty-one members of LANE have not even met each other. However, since no member was farther than distance two from the president of the organization, the maximum distance between any two members was four. The average distance was slightly less than two, so that the proximity score was .52.

The transitivity score was a similarly moderate .48. Retired persons in LANE had a large amount of allocable time, very little of which went to LANE activities. Accordingly, their frequency scores were very low. The observer thought that several of them were capable of and willing to make contributions of talent and energy, but were ignored by the rather patronizing president. It was rumored that the president was having an affair with the housewife who was most active in the organization. More in reaction to the favoritism he showed her than to the affair itself, most of the other housewives limited their involvement. Nonetheless, since they had so little time to allocate, their frequency scores were substantially higher than for retired persons, in most cases. The unit-wide frequency score was .27.

Some members of LANE belonged to no other organizations with interactive activities during the summer of observation. This was a key factor in the relatively high scope score of .41. LANE has absolutely no barrier to membership beyond a nominal contribution, which is waived upon request. Thus, its impermeability score is 0.

Collectively, the five group predicates yield a group score of .34 for LANE.

Over all six activities, there were only thirteen roles in LANE. The average number occupied by any individual member during the course of the summer was 2.8. Thus, the specialization score was .79. Since there is scarcely any interchanging of roles, the asymmetry score was .88.

The president of LANE awarded roles to members based on what he imagined were their external backgrounds. His blatant prejudices annoyed most of the members. For instance, he tried to appoint one woman with acting experience to raise funds door-to-door, with the explanation that he knew members of local theater groups who do that. He managed to keep his office by reminding the members that he was the only one who was qualified to present their case to the NRC. The observer thought that for LANE, nearly all roles were ascribed on the basis of established categories. The entltlement score was .82.

The only sanction at the leader's disposal was disapproval, which he expressed with varying degrees of pompous sarcasm. Since LANE is a voluntary organization, he certainly could not assign undesirable work. When he tried to expel one of the high-school students, she snapped that the bylaws which he himself had foisted on the membership made no provision for expulsion. She quit LANE and joined the Scallopshell Caucus. The infrequency of accountability interactions led to an accountability score of .23.

These four predicate scores led to a net grid score of .68 for LANE.

Scallopshell Caucus

The nineteen members of the Scallopshell Caucus actively sought contact with each other, subordinating personal likes and dislikes to their common goals. Their general meetings were frequent, and usually all members were present. Nearly every evening, some of them would hang out at a local beer and pizza restaurant. Every member was involved in every activity. Their EXACT graph was complete, implying a proximity score and a transitivity score of 1.0.

Most of the activities of the members of the caucus are self-explanatory. Their most conspicuous act of civil disobedience was a symbolic occupation of the proposed reactor site on Hiroshima day in early August. Activities of the Scallopshell Caucus were:

General meetings
Leaflet distribution
Fundraising
NRC licensing hearings
Alternative energy fairs
Membership inductions
Nonviolent civil disobedience
Small political gatherings (informal parties)
Beer and pizza hangout

Like other social units, they have frequent small gatherings that might be described as informal parties, except that the word "party" was too frivolous a connotation to be acceptable. The observer was coldly informed that the gatherings were political meetings. She was invited to only one of them.

The only activities outside their unit that Scallops allowed themselves were of an educational nature. Several were formally enrolled in programs of study at a nearby community college. Others attended YMCA classes in things like carpentry and folk-dancing. The unit-wide frequency and scope scores were .89 and .91, respectively.

Four persons tried to join the Scallopshell Caucus during the summer the observer was present. One was inducted shortly before Labor Day, but the other three were refused on the grounds of insufficient commitment. Thus, the impermeability score was .75.

The Scallopshell Caucus scored high in every one of the five predicates of group. Their aggregate group score was .91.

In principle, every member assumed every role. Had the period of observation been longer, the specialization score would almost certainly have been 0, rather than the value of .12 actually observed. Since each activity had only one role, there was perfect symmetry. There were no ascribed roles. While members often expressed personal disapproval of each other's actions, there were no role-based sanctions. Accordingly, the scores for asymmetry, entitlement, and accountability were all 0.

These low scores in every grid predicate yielded an aggregate grid score of .03.

The predicate scores of all five social units at Lakemouth are shown in table 6.1. Figure 6.3 shows the location of each unit's coordinates in the grid/group diagram. It may be observed that these measured values are consistent with our predictions in chapter 3 (see figure 3.1).

Because this is a toy example, the match between the two diagrams comes as no surprise. However, we might anticipate that, in real cases, some social units do not turn out to be where

Table 6.1. Summary of Predicate Scores and Composite Grid/ Group Scores

	Chamber of Commerce	Local 387	Dunes Dwellers	LANE	Scallop-shell Caucus
prox	.97	.48	.56	.52	1.0
trans	.90	.88	.16	.48	1.0
freq	.52	.37	.07	.27	.89
scope	.72	.94	.20	.41	.91
imper	.85	.11	n/a	0	.75
Group	.79	.56	.25	.34	.91
spec	.90	.92	0	.79	.12
asym	.88	.89	.14	.88	0
entitle	.97	.26	0	.82	0
acc	.23	.95	0	.23	0
Grid	.75	.76	.035	.68	.03

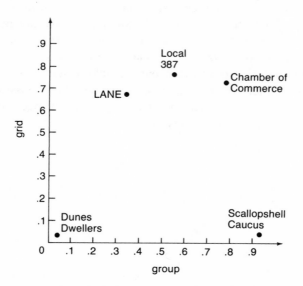

Figure 6.3. Grid/group diagram for the social units involved in the Lakemouth controversy

a qualitative assessment would put them. This is because qualitative assignment of a unit to a particular grid/group cell is based on comparison to a stereotypical description of the appropriate ideal type. But, different investigators may assess proximity to a stereotype differently. Furthermore, it is easy to miss counter-evidence. For example, a unit that appears to have extensive behavioral rules would be assigned to high grid if the investigator is unaware that the rules system allows substitution for, and exceptions to, the prescribed conduct. Our measurement of behavior is less prone to such errors. The quantitive analysis in figure 6.3 is therefore a more reliable representation of the facts than figure 3.1. as well as being reproducible with less contention.

Figure 6.3 has the further advantage of enabling one to discriminate between units within the same quadrant. This might prove to be useful in comparing the completeness of a cosmology in a social unit, the effectiveness of its perceptual filters, or even the degree of conviction with which its tenets are adhered to. Units that are adjacent to another cosmological type might prove to be more susceptible to the ideas and examples of the neighboring type than those of other, more distant, types. Units that are close to another type of social context may also have a greater ability to borrow rhetoric from an adjacent cosmology than units located in the far corners of the diagram. However, these possibilities remain topics for empirical investigation. Our strongest claims remain those of reproducibility and reliability.

CHAPTER SEVEN

CONCLUSIONS

If this study were of a real town, we would hope to draw some unanticipated conclusions about the nuclear power controversy from it. However, it would be spurious for us to offer specific advice to planners about what kinds of communities are likely to shun these particular projects, or what kinds of new technologies are likely to prove unacceptable to large sections of the public, on the basis of the Lakemouth data. Lakemouth is a fictitious example, and our conclusions could not be put to the test.

Therefore, if our readers expect us to pull a rabbit from the hat at this point, we hope they will not be disappointed to find that we are trapeze artists rather than conjurers. Our object has not been to surprize the reader with the originality of our conclusions, but to display our striving for precision in full view of the audience. To this end, we have described a paradigm for cultural analysis that we hope will be taken up, tested, and developed in the course of empirical research by others as well as ourselves.

We have described a method for establishing a predictable linkage between social organizations and culture. Throughout, we have adopted a view of culture as the ideational, symbolic, attitudinal, and behavioral patterns that enable people to make sense of and deal with the organizational frameworks they encounter. It is in this sense that we call culture a programming mechanism, or a means of social accounting.

This view of culture, especially the hypothesis that there is a limited number of basic culture types, first began to crystallize in the work of Benedict (1934). Douglas (1980) has drawn a social accounting approach out of the work of Evans-Pritchard, although her emphasis on this element in his wide-ranging contributions to anthropological theory has proved controversial. But, it is not contestable that complementary interpretations of culture as programming on accounting mechanisms for social units have appeared in the writings of contemporary anthropologists. This view of culture receives its most formal expression in the writings of Mary Douglas, who originated grid/group analysis. It is also an important component in the work of Clifford Geertz (1973), although his is a more literary approach, relying on what he calls "thick description" in preference to the mathematical modeling that we are proposing.

We hope that the present work has made a fourfold contribution to this developing tradition. First, we have attempted to provide a general model for the organizational component of cultural analysis. We have explicitly advocated rendering social organizations as diverse as bureaucracies, political and religious bodies, tribal and family groups as mathematically modeled *social units*.

Second, we have applied *polythetic scales* to the measurement of the multiple-hierarchy (grid) and social-network (group) aspects of that model. The extent of our debt to organization theorists and network analysts is a topic in itself and has not been developed here. What is new is that we have demonstrated a paradigm for simultaneously quantifying the differences in both aspects of social organization. Furthermore, we claim that measurements made in this way can be replicated by different researchers, thus establishing for the first time the empirical basis for falsifying grid/group analysis. If, on the other hand, the theory withstands the test, we should have a surer basis for both the synchronic comparison of different social units and diachronic changes in the same unit than has existed hitherto.

Third, we have provided the means to resolve empirically some of the speculative controversies about the model that cannot be decided by theoretical debate. For example, it is not yet clear how actual patterns of belief and behavior superimpose on the four-quadrant grid/group diagram shown in figure 1.1. Rayner (1979) has suggested that quadrants A, B, C, and D may be iden-

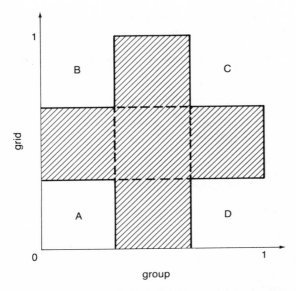

Figure 7.1. **Correspondence of quadrants A, B, C, and D to extreme regions of the continuous grid/group diagram**

tified with the extreme regions of the continuous grid/group diagram, as shown in figure 7.1. According to this interpretation, social units located in the regions of medium grid and group strength are likely to exhibit the cosmology of the prototype to which they are closest, but in a form modified by the adjacent cosmology. Rayner gives examples of creeping social change from one model of organization to another, as well as cases where it appears quite suddenly, as the accumulation of small unnoticed changes in an established social system overdetermines it in the direction of a new organizational prototype and accompanying cosmology.

Thompson (1982a,b) however, rejects the possibility of smooth transition from one prototype to another. He fills the space in the center of the diagram with a fifth region, of autonomous social organization with its own distinctive cosmology, as shown in

SURVIVAL INDIVIDUALIST   +
Little developed but eclectic.
Passivity.
Wild views on abroad.
Little developed time perspective.
Erratic child-rearing (alternating
    between indulgence and
    violence).
Millennialism.
Anomic suicide.

MANIPULATIVE COLLECTIVIST
Transcendental metaphysics (society and nature
    isomorphous).
Ritualist (ensures proper harmony between society
    and nature).
Natural law.
Cautious about abroad.
Sacrifice. Strong on tradition.
Tough discipline/child training.
Altruistic suicide.

AUTONOMOUS
Nature mysticism (nature and society as one).
Simplicity and naturalness valued.
Approves of abroad. Live in present.
Natural goodness of children (progressive
    theory of education).
As yet unidentified type of suicide?

−   +

MANIPULATIVE INDIVIDUALIST
Nature and society separate
    ("every prospect pleases and
    only man is vile").
Intellectual rigor. High standards.
    High culture.
Looks to autonomy in
    unthreatened moments (so
    progressive theory of
    education but with hidden
    controls).
Frantically in favor of abroad.
Strong (manipulative) sense of
    history.
Egotistic suicide.   −

SURVIVAL COLLECTIVIST
Homespun philosophy ("small is beautiful").
Us (vulnerable) v. Them (predatory).
Scapegoating (denatured humans).
Poison. Contamination. Purge
Witchcraft accusations.
Tough discipline/child training.
Xenophobic.
Strong on tradition.
Fatalistic suicide.

Figure 7.2. Thompson's discontinuous grid/group diagram.

figure 7.2. According to this interpretation social change from
one grid/group prototype to another will appear to be a sharp
transition at the interface of adjacent cosmologies.

Fourth, we have illustrated, through the invention of the comprehensive Lakemouth example, the potential usefulness of this
method of measuring culture to important public-policy issues,
such as the choice and location of hazardous technologies. Part
of our aim has been to contribute to a wider effort to rescue the

concept of culture from an artifactual consideration, taken seriously only by anthropologists. We have sought to provide the experimental basis to test the proposition advanced by Douglas and Wildavsky (1982) that the concept of culture should occupy a central role in understanding peoples' attitudes toward the vital issues of modern society.

We believe that there is a pressing need for empirical research built upon the sort of paradigm we are offering. It remains to be tested in the fields of political science, sociology, public policy and public health, risk analysis, industrial relations, family counseling, and many others. But we anticipate that quantitative grid/group analysis will become a common method in many branches of social research, as it is increasingly recognized that understanding people's attitudes and ideas about the world are as important as understanding their economic positions.

Obviously, the method we have outlined is expensive of time and resources and is therefore principally applicable to small-scale social units. We have eschewed the use of questionnaires for gathering data from people about their social organization because of the problem of circularity. If people's ideas about the world and their place in it are influenced by their experience of social organizations then they will report their own social organization from that same standpoint.

However, once the method for establishing the correlation between cosmology and social experience that we have described here has been tested, the development of survey techniques for grid/group analysis may be opened up. It should be possible to construct questionnaires to elicit self-reported aspects of people's cosmologies that we know from experiments with small-scale social units are correlated with particular organizational configurations. On the basis of the answers to these questions it should be possible to allocate respondents to their respective grid/group categories and, on this basis, predict other aspects of their cosmology that we have not asked about. To test the validity of this approach, it should be possible to refrain from asking some questions in a first-stage questionnaire, then predict the answers before examining the second stage in which those questions are asked. If the correlation is good enough, then the mass summary approach would be justified. However, much work using the small-scale technique we have described here is necessary before we can begin to develop such a mass summary application of grid/group analysis.

A COMPUTER PROGRAM TO CALCULATE GRID/GROUP SCORES

This appendix lists a computer program, written in standard BASIC, to calculate the values of grid/group predicates from experimental data. It also contains instructions for using the program. If your computer system is nonstandard, you might have to modify some of the program statements.

```
                  >>>>        *  PROGRAM  *          <<<<
00100   rem ********************* DECLARATIONS *************************
00110   rem-- declarations for vectors and arrays ...  These are defined
00120   rem-- either by 'size' or by 'size'*'maxRoles'  (see below)
00130      rem
00140      rem *****  predicate vectors  *****
00150         dim distsum(20), trans(20), freq(20), scope(20), asym(20)
00160         dim spec(20), entitle(20), acc(20)
00170      rem
00180      rem *****  associated node information  *****
00190         dim nodename$(20), outact(20), S(20), valence(20)
00200      rem
00210      rem *****  basic graph-structure info  *****
00220         dim adjmat(20,20), adjset(20,20)
00230         dim apsp(20,20), dummy(20,20), pairasym(20,20), Dom(20,20)
00240      rem
00250      rem *****  vectors of input information  *****
00260         dim name1int$(400), name2int$(400), role1int$(400)
00270         dim role2int$(400), diffroles$(400), roles$(400)
00280         dim interactions$(400), roletype$(400)
00290      rem
00300   size = 20                   ! Max. declared size of member matrices etc.
00310   maxRoles = 20               ! presumed maximum # of roles per member
00320   bigsize = maxRoles*size     ! Max. size of role and interaction arrays
00330   EndData$ = 'END'            ! Signals End-of-Data of data block
00340   rem
00350   rem
00360   rem ********************* MAINLINE ****************************
00370      rem  *****  read data from input file and prettyprint it  *****
00380         gosub 1120            ! Store the interactions-- members & activities
00390         gosub 810             ! Print out interactions
00400         gosub 910             ! Print out 'key' to adjacency matrices
00410      rem
00420      rem
00430      rem *** Calculate and print group predicates ***
00440      print 'Group Predicates:'
00450         gosub 4200           !      All-Pairs Shortest Path matrix
00460         gosub 1550           !      'Proximity' predicate
00470         gosub 1780           !      'Transitivity' predicate
00480         gosub 2170           !      'Frequency' predicate
00490         gosub 2350           !      'Scope' predicate
00500         gosub 2590           !      'Impermeability' predicate
00510      print
00520      rem *** Calculate and print grid predicates ***
00530      print 'Grid Predicates:'
00540         gosub 2760           !      'Specialization' predicate
00550         gosub 3150           !      'Asymmetry' predicate
00560         gosub 3760           !      'Entitlement' predicate
00570         gosub 4000           !      'Accountability' predicate
00580   rem-- END OF MAINLINE
00590   rem
00600   rem-- Technical section: print out assorted matrices
00610         gosub 4440                 ! Initialise Display Matrix
00620         print 'adjcency matrix: '
00630         mat dummy = adjmat
00640         gosub 4530                 ! Print adjacency matrix
00650         print 'set of adjacencies: '
00660         mat dummy = adjset
```

```
00670          gosub 4530              ! Print set of adjacencies
00680          print 'A-P SP  Matrix'
00690          mat dummy = apsp
00700          gosub 4530              ! Print 'Distance' matrix
00710          rem
00720          rem-- end of technical section
00730          rem
00740     close 1                      ! Close input file
00750     stop
00760          rem
00770          rem
00780          rem-- SUBROUTINES
00790          rem
00800     rem ****************** PRETTYPRINT DISPLAY ********************
00810     rem-- Subroutine prints out list of interactions
00820          print 'The interaction-activities  represented in the graph: '
00830          print
00840          for k = 1 to bigsize
00850             print  interactions$(k)
00860             if interactions$(k) = "" then goto 880
00870             next k
00880          print
00890          return
00900          rem
00910     rem-- Subroutine maps the names of people onto adjmatrix label of node
00920          print
00930          gosub 1030                              ! Calculate numpeople
00940          print ' # of people modeled in the graph is: '; numpeople
00950          for i = 1 to numpeople
00960             print 'Label ';i ;' represents person:  ';nodename$(i)
00970             next i
00980          print
00990          return
01000          rem
01010     rem *****  END  OF PRETTYPRINT DISPLAY  *****
01020     rem *****  DETERMINATION OF # OF NODES IN GRAPH  *****
01030     rem-- Subroutine determines the number of nodes in the graph
01040          for i = 1 to size
01050             if nodename$(i) = "" goto 1070           ! find first empty cell
01060             next i
01070          numpeople = i -1
01080          return
01090          rem
01100     rem      *****  END OF NODE NUMBER DETERMINATION  *****
01110     rem ***********  PRINCIPLE GRAPH-STRUCTURE DATA ENTRY  *************
01120     rem-- Subroutine reads in the list of interactions between members.
01130     rem-- The information is stored in the app. data structures.
01140          j = 0
01150          open "info.dat" for input as file 1
01160          input #1, name1$, name2$
01170          input #1,  role1$, acc1$, role2$,acc2$, wt12, wt21
01180          if name1$ = EndData$ then goto 1500  ! end of data
01190          name$ = name1$
01200          gosub 4870                     ! Find Label for the member/node
01210          if space = 0 then print "error-- too little space in array DS"
01220          row = code                     ! Found app. row in adjmat
01230          xrole$ = role1$
01240          gosub 4740                     ! Enter role in Diffroles list
01250          name$ = name2$
01260          gosub 4870                     ! Find Label for the member/node
```

```
01270        if space = 0 then print "error-- too little space in array DS"
01280        column = code                          ! Found app. column in adjmat
01290        xrole$ = role2$
01300        gosub 4740                      ! Enter role in Diffroles List
01310        if adjmat(row, column) < wt12 then adjmat(row, column) = wt12
01320        if adjmat(column, row) < wt21 then adjmat(column, row) = wt21
01330        adjset (row, column) = adjset (row, column) +1
01340        adjset (column, row) = adjset (column, row) +1
01350        if ( ((acc1$='D')and(acc2$='S')) or ((acc1$='S')and(acc2$='D')) )&
             then goto 1370
01360        goto 1400                       ! Interaction is not a dom-sub. one
01370   rem-- Update matrix of dominant-subordinate roles
01380        Dom(row,column) = Dom(row,column) +1
01390        Dom(column,row) = Dom(column,row) +1
01400        wt12$ = '1'                      ! For purposes of data storage we
01410        wt21$ = '1'                      ! assume all weights = 1
01420        if (j=size*maxRoles) then print 'Out of space in interaction arrays&
             -- Error!!'
01430        j = j +1                        ! Store the interaction info
01440        interactions$(j) = '[' +name1$ +' / ' +name2$+ ']' +' <'+ role1$&
             +' <=> '+role2$ +'> ' + '[' +wt12$ +'|' +wt21$ +']'
01450        name1int$(j) = name1$
01460        name2int$(j) = name2$
01470        role1int$(j) = role1$
01480        role2int$(j) = role2$
01490        goto 1160                       ! loop to read more data
01500        return
01510        rem
01520   rem ************* END OF PRINCIPLE DATA ENTRY *****************
01530   rem ********************** PREDICATES SECTION ***********************
01540   rem                    ***** GROUP PREDICATES ****
01550   rem ********************* PROXIMITY PREDICATE  **********************
01560        for i = 1 to numpeople
01570           sum = 0
01580           for j = 1 to numpeople
01590              sum = sum + apsp(j,i) ! sum = Summ. of row 'i' in matrix apsp
01600              next j
01610           distsum (i) = sum
01620           next i
01630        for i = 1 to numpeople
01640           distsum (i) = distsum (i) /(numpeople -1)
01650           if distsum (i) <> 0 then distsum (i) = 1/distsum (i)
01660           next i
01670        proximity = 0
01680        for i = 1 to numpeople
01690           proximity = proximity + distsum (i)
01700           next i
01710        proximity = proximity/numpeople
01720        print '----------------------------------------------'
01730        print 'PROXIMITY PREDICATE:  '; proximity
01740        print '----------------------------------------------'
01750        return
01760        rem
01770   rem ******************* TRANSITIVITY PREDICATE  *******************
01780   rem-- Subroutine calculates array 'trans' where trans(i) represents
01790   rem-- the ratio of complete triples containing 'i' to the number of
01800   rem-- connected triples containing 'i'
01810        for i = 1 to numpeople
01820           conn = 0                   ! Initialise # of connected triples
01830           comp = 0                   ! Initialise # of complete triples
```

```
01840                for j = 1 to i
01850                    for k = j +1 to numpeople
01860                        if adjmat (j,k) = 0 then goto 2000   ! next k
01870                        for l = k +1 to numpeople
01880                            if j <> i  goto 1920
01890                            if adjmat (k,1)>0 or adjmat (j,1)>0 then conn = conn +1
01900                            if adjmat (k,1)>0 and adjmat (j,1)>0 then comp =comp +1
01910                            goto 1990                         ! next l
01920                            if k <> i  goto 1960
01930                            if adjmat (k,1)>0 or adjmat (j,1)>0 then conn = conn +1
01940                            if adjmat (k,1)>0 and adjmat (j,1)>0 then comp =comp +1
01950                            goto 1990                         ! next l
01960                            if l <> i goto 1990               ! next l
01970                            if adjmat (k,1)>0 or adjmat (j,1)>0 then conn =conn +1
01980                            if adjmat (k,1)>0 and  adjmat (j,1)>0 then comp=comp +1
01990                        next l
02000                    next k
02010                next j
02020            trans (i) = comp/conn
02030            print 'trans # '; i; ' = '; trans (i)
02040            next i
02050        for i = 1 to numpeople          ! Calculate transitivity predicate
02060            transitivity = trans (i) + transitivity
02070            next i
02080        transitivity = transitivity/numpeople
02090        print '--------------------------------------------'
02100        print 'TRANSITIVITY PREDICATE:  '; transitivity
02110        print '--------------------------------------------'
02120        print
02130        print
02140        return
02150        rem
02160    rem ****************** FREQUENCY PREDICATE  ************************
02170    rem-- Subroutine calculates frequency predicate based on stored data
02180        input #1, namex$, tottime, acttime      ! Read interaction time/person
02190        if namex$ = EndData$ then goto 2240      ! End-of-Data
02200        name$ = namex$                           ! Assign to dummy variable
02210        gosub 4660                               ! Find node label for name
02220        freq(label) = acttime/tottime
02230        goto 2180                                ! Loop for more data
02240        for i = 1 to numpeople
02250            frequency = freq(i) + frequency
02260            print 'freq '; i; ' = '; freq(i)
02270            next i
02280        frequency = frequency/numpeople
02290        print '--------------------------------------------'
02300        print ' FREQUENCY PREDICATE:  '; frequency
02310        print '--------------------------------------------'
02320        return
02330        rem
02340    rem ****************** SCOPE PREDICATE  ****************************
02350    rem-- Subroutine calculates Scope predicate based on stored data
02360    rem-- Scope (i) = # of inter-unit activities/total # of activities
02370        for i = 1 to numpeople              ! first get inter-unit activ.
02380            for j = 1 to numpeople
02390                scope(i) = scope(i) + adjset(i,j)
02400                next j
02410            next i
02420        input #1, name$, activity$               ! read the outside activities
02430        if name$ = EndData$ then goto 2470       ! End-of-Data
```

```
02440        gosub 4660                              ! Get person's node label
02450        outact (label) = outact(label) +1       ! person has an out unit activ.
02460        goto 2420                               ! Loop for more data
02470        for i = 1 to numpeople
02480            scope(i) = scope(i)/(scope(i) +outact(i))
02490            print 'scope '; i; ' = '; scope(i)
02500            scopepred = scopepred + scope(i)
02510            next i
02520        scopepred = scopepred/numpeople
02530        print '--------------------------------------------'
02540        print 'SCOPE PREDICATE:  ', scopepred
02550        print '--------------------------------------------'
02560        return
02570        rem
02580    rem ****************** IMPERMEABILITY PREDICATE *******************
02590    rem-- Subroutine determines Impermeability predicate:  [Entry ratio
02600    rem-- = #eligible members who join/#eligible members who want to join]
02610        input #1, person$, join$               ! list of eligible non-members
02620        if person$ = EndData$ then goto 2670   ! End-of-Data
02630        if join$ = 'N' then goto 2650          ! Person not allowed to join
02640        numjoined = numjoined +1
02650        total = total +1
02660        goto 2610                              ! Loop for more data
02670        Entry = numjoined/total                ! Entry Ratio
02680        Impermeability = 1  -Entry
02690        print '--------------------------------------------'
02700        print 'IMPERMEABILITY PREDICATE:  '; Impermeability
02710        print '--------------------------------------------'
02720        return
02730        rem
02740    rem            *****  GRID PREDICATES  *****
02750    rem ****************** SPECIALIZATION PREDICATE *******************
02760    rem-- Subroutine determines Specialization Predicate; C = total #
02770    rem-- of roles in unit, S(i) = # roles assumed by node 'i'
02780        i = 0
02790        i = i +1
02800        input #1, roles$(i), roletype$(i)      ! Read list of roles
02810        if roles$(i) = EndData$ goto 2830      ! End-of-Data
02820        goto 2790                              ! Loop for more data
02830        numroles = i -1                        ! 'C' is now determined
02840        for i = 1 to numroles                            ! Calculate 'S(i)'
02850            rem-- The idea is to compare each role on role list with the
02860            rem-- interaction lists: how many people assume that role?
02870            xrole$ = roles$(i)
02880                rem-- Determine whether either of the roles in interaction
02890                rem-- = xrole; if so add role to list of roles per person.
02900                gosub 3050                     ! Try to update 'S(member)'
02910            next i                             ! Try next role
02920        for i = 1 to numpeople
02930            Spec (i) = 1 - (S(i)/numroles)
02940            print 'Spec '; i ;' = '; Spec(i)
02950            next i
02960        for i = 1 to numpeople
02970            Specialization = Specialization + Spec(i)
02980            next i
02990        Specialization = Specialization/numpeople
03000        print '--------------------------------------------'
03010        print 'SPECIALIZATION PREDICATE:  '; Specialization
03020        print '--------------------------------------------'
03030        return
```

```
03040      rem
03050  rem-- Subroutine determines whether any member of an interaction
03060  rem-- assumes xrole; if yes update S(member)
03070      for l = 1 to numpeople
03080         code = 1
03090         gosub 5000                          ! Does member #'code' assume xrole$ ?
03100         if valid = 1 then S(code) = S(code) +1
03110         next l                                      ! Check out next member
03120      return
03130      rem
03140  rem ****************** ASYMMETRY PREDICATE ************************
03150  rem-- Subroutine calculates Asymmetry predicate as 'asym (i)';
03160  rem-- pairasym(i,j) represents # of 1-way roles between i and j
03170      for i = 1 to numpeople              ! All i,j that do not interact
03180         for j = 1 to numpeople           ! have an undefined pair score
03190            if adjmat (i,j) = 0 then pairasym (i,j) = -1
03200            next j
03210         next i
03220      for i = 1 to bigsize
03230         if namelint$(i) = "" then goto 3460     ! No more interactions
03240         oneway = 1                        ! Assume that int. is 1-way
03250         name$ = namelint$(i)
03260         gosub 4660                              ! Find label of that name
03270         lab1 = label
03280         name$ = name2int$(i)
03290         gosub 4660                              ! Find label of 2nd name
03300         lab2 = label
03310         rem-- Systematically scan the lists of interactions for any 1-way
03320         rem-- role pairs for lab1,lab2.  If any exist, add to contents
03330         rem-- of pairasym(lab1,lab2);
03340         for j = 1 to bigsize
03350            if namelint$(j) = "" then goto 3400     ! No more interactions
03360            rem-- Spot int. that are NOT 1-way role pairs; SKIP them.
03370            if ((namelint$(i)=name2int$(j)) and (name2int$(i)&
                   =namelint$(j)) and (rolelint$(i)=role1int$(j)) and&
                   (role2int$(i)=role2int$(j)) )  then goto 3410
03380            if ( (namelint$(i)=namelint$(j)) and (name2int$(i)&
                   =name2int$(j)) and (rolelint$(i)=role2int$(j)) and&
                   (role2int$(i)=rolelint$(j)) ) then goto 3410
03390            next j
03400         goto 3420                               ! Int. is 1-way
03410         oneway = 0                              ! Int. is not 1-way
03420         rem-- If found, add one to the # of 1-way role pairs per int.
03430         if oneway <> 0 then pairasym(lab1,lab2) = pairasym(lab1,lab2) +1
03440         if oneway <> 0 then pairasym(lab2,lab1) = pairasym(lab2,lab1) +1
03450         next i                                  ! get next interaction
03460      rem-- Calculate Valence(i)--  # of members with which 'i' interacts
03470      for i = 1 to numpeople
03480         for j = 1 to numpeople
03490            if adjmat(i,j) >0 then valence(i) = valence(i) +1
03500            next j
03510         next i
03520      rem-- Determine ratio of 1-way roles i >=j : total # of int. i >=j
03530      for i = 1 to numpeople
03540         for j = 1 to numpeople
03550            if (pairasym(i,j) >=0)&
                   then pairasym(i,j) = pairasym(i,j)/adjset(i,j)
03560            next j
03570         next i
03580      for i = 1 to numpeople
```

```
03590          sum = 0
03600          for j = 1 to numpeople
03610             if (pairasym(i,j) >=0) then sum = pairasym(i,j) + sum
03620             next j
03630          asym(i) = sum/valence(i)
03640          print 'asym '; i; '= '; asym(i)
03650          next i
03660       for i = 1 to numpeople
03670          asymmetry = asymmetry + asym(i)
03680          next i
03690       asymmetry = asymmetry/numpeople
03700       print '-----------------------------------------'
03710       print 'ASYMMETRY PREDICATE:  '; asymmetry
03720       print '-----------------------------------------'
03730       return
03740       rem
03750    rem ****************** ENTITLEMENT PREDICATE *********************
03760    rem-- Subroutine calculates Entitlement predicate
03770       for i = 1 to numpeople
03780          for j = 1 to numroles
03790             xrole$ = roles$(j)
03800             code = i
03810             gosub 5000                        ! Member 'code' assume xrole?
03820             if valid = 0 goto 3840 ! Member does not assume xrole
03830             if roletype$(j)='asc' then entitle(i)=entitle(i) +1 ! asc role
03840             next j
03850          next i
03860       for i = 1 to numpeople
03870          entitle(i) = entitle(i)/S(i)
03880          print 'entitle '; i; ' ='; entitle(i)
03890          next i
03900       for i = 1 to numpeople
03910          entitlement = entitlement + entitle(i)
03920          next i
03930       entitlement = entitlement/numpeople
03940       print '-----------------------------------------'
03950       print 'ENTITLEMENT PREDICATE:  '; entitlement
03960       print '-----------------------------------------'
03970       return
03980       rem
03990    rem **************** ACCOUNTABILITY PREDICATE ********************
04000    rem-- Subroutine determines Accountability predicate.
04010       for i = 1 to numpeople
04020          sum = 0
04030          for j = 1 to  numpeople
04040             sum = Dom(i,j) +sum
04050             next j
04060          acc(i) = sum/valence(i)
04070          print 'accountability '; i; ' = '; acc(i)
04080          next i
04090       for i = 1 to numpeople
04100          accountability = acc(i) + accountability
04110          next i
04120       accountability = accountability/numpeople
04130       print '-----------------------------------------'
04140       print 'ACCOUNTABILITY PREDICATE:  ';accountability
04150       print '-----------------------------------------'
04160       return
04170       rem
04180    rem **************** END OF PREDICATES SECTION ********************
```

```
04190    rem *****   Calculation of All-Pairs Shortest Path Matrix  *****
04200    rem-- Subroutine calculates the shortest path matrix apsp given a
04210    rem-- cost matrix 'adjmat'.  [Uses Floyd's algorithm]
04220       infinity = 1000000                    ! artificial high constant
04230       for i = 0 to size
04240          for j = 0 to size
04250             apsp (i,j) = adjmat (i,j)
04260             if adjmat (i,j) = 0 then apsp (i,j) = infinity
04270             next j
04280        next i
04290        for i = 1 to size
04300           apsp (i,i) = 0
04310           next i
04320        for i = 1 to size
04330           for j = 1 to size
04340              for k = 1 to size
04350                 if apsp(j,i)+apsp(i,k) < apsp(j,k)&
                          then apsp(j,k) = apsp(j,i)+apsp(i,k)
04360                    next k
04370                 next j
04380              next i
04390           return
04400           rem
04410    rem              *****  End of APSP Calculation  *****
04420    rem
04430    rem              *****  'Display' Matrix Primitives  *****
04440    rem-- Subroutine initialises display matrix to label rows and columns
04450        for i = 1 to  size   ! BASIC initialises the matrices to 0 matrix
04460           dummy (i,0) = i
04470           for j = 1 to size
04480              dummy (0,j) = j
04490              next j
04500           next i
04510        return
04520        rem
04530    rem-- Subroutine prints matrix 'dummy' in packed format
04540        for i = 0 to numpeople
04550           for j = 0 to numpeople
04560              print dummy (i,j);
04570              next j
04580           print
04590           next i
04600        print
04610        print
04620        return
04630        rem
04640    rem  ***********************************************************
04650    rem  ******************** PROGRAM PRIMITIVES  ********************
04660    rem-- Subroutine returns the node label given the name of unit-member
04670        for n = 1 to numpeople
04680           if nodename$(n) = name$ then label = n
04690           if nodename$(n) = name$ goto 4720         ! Return label
04700           next n
04710        print '!! ';name$; ' not listed in interaction input, check file '
04720        return
04730        rem
04740    rem-- Subroutine enters the SET (no duplicates) of roles assumed
04750    rem-- by member #'code' in cells code*maxRoles -(maxRoles+1)
04760    rem-- of Diffroles. [maxRoles cells]
04770        low = (code*maxRoles) +(-maxRoles +1)
```

```
04780        high = (code*maxRoles)
04790        for s = low to high
04800            if Diffroles$(s) = "" goto 4840        ! Empty cell for storage
04810            if Diffroles$(s) = xrole$ goto 4850    ! role already stored
04820        next s
04830        if (s=high) and (Diffroles$(s)<>xrole$) then print 'Diffroles array&
                 out of space-- needs to be enlarged'
04840        Diffroles$(s) = xrole$
04850        return
04860        rem
04870    rem-- Subroutine determines whether a node already exists in the graph.
04880    rem-- If not, the name is entered; if yes, label of node is returned.
04890        space = 1                     ! there is space in DS to enter name
04900        code = 0                      ! label of node in adj matrix
04910        for i = 1 to size
04920            if nodename$(i) = "" then goto 4950      ! name not yet in graph
04930            if nodename$(i) = name$ then goto 4950   ! name is in graph
04940        next i
04950        code = i
04960        if nodename$(i)<>name$ and i = 35 then space = 0 ! DS ran out space
04970        nodename$(i) = name$
04980        return
04990        rem
05000    rem-- Subroutine determines whether role xrole$ is assumed by member
05010    rem-- #'code' by checking the cells in Diffroles array
05020        valid = 0                                ! role not found
05030        low = (code*maxRoles) +(-maxRoles +1)
05040        high = (code*maxRoles)
05050        for q = low to high
05060            if Diffroles$(q) = xrole$ goto 5090
05070        next q
05080        goto 5100
05090        valid = 1                                ! role found
05100        return
05110        rem
99999    end
```

- -

```
                         ***   INPUT   ***

        Before attempting to run the program (by creating an input file)
you must do a preliminary ethnography.  This preliminary work will be the basis
of the input file, and will also serve as a check for later work.


*** Format of the Preliminary Ethnography ***

"*** Society Structure ***"
"Membership List"
    1. member1
    2. member2
    .

    .

    .


"Activity List and Roles"
    1. activity1
         1. role1 (ach or asc)
         2. role2 (ach or asc)
         .

         .

         .

    2. activity2
         1. role1 (ach or asc)
         2. role2 (ach or asc)
         .

         .

         .

    3. activity3
    .

    .

    .


"Eligible Nonmembers"
    1. eligible1
    2. eligible2
    .

    .

    .


*** Format of the Data Sample ***

"*** Sample ***"
"Observed Activity Sequence"
    1. observed activity1
         1. role-pair interaction1   (acc or not)
         2. role-pair interaction2   (acc or not)
         .

         .

         .

    2. observed activity2
         1. role-pair interaction1   (acc or not)
```

2. role-pair interaction2 (acc or not)
.
.
.

.
.
.
.

"Observed Time Allocations"
    1. member1
        allocable time1, interactive time1
        # inside activities1, # wholly external activities1
    2. member2
        allocable time2, interactive time2
        # inside activities2, # wholly external activities2
    .
    .
    .

"Eligibles Who Became Members"
    1. newmember1
    2. newmember2
    .
    .
    .

*** FILE PREPARATION   ***

        At this point you have completed your preliminary ethnography. In
order for the program to run you must create an input file, called 'info.dat'.
We will first give details as to the construction of this file, and then give
a sample file with the program execution on that file.

        The data must be recorded in the following format into a file named
info.dat that the computer will read to calculate the predicates. Clearly
a lot of data are involved. The program has been constructed with the
objectives of keeping the error rate to a minimum and of keeping the time and
effort of file preparation low.

*** DETAILS OF PROGRAM INPUT ***

        Your input must contain five blocks of information. At the end of
each block, to signify End-of-Input, an additional line should be written
containing the same # of info as the rest of that block. The first piece
MUST be the signal 'END'. The rest can be anything, although things are
clearer if they are also 'END' (or '0' for numerical information).

*** BLOCK 1 ***
        For each role-pair interaction, two lines of input must be supplied.
This must contain

Line1>>
        1: name1

```
        2:    name2
Line2>>
        3:    role1
        4:    asc1?
        5:    role2
        6:    asc2?
        7:    weight1=>2
        8:    weight2=>1
```

where

    role1 = the role that name1 assumes during the interaction
    role2 = the role that name2 assumes during the interaction
    asc1? indicates whether role1 is dominant or subordinate to role2
    asc2? indicates whether role2 is dominant or subordinate to role1

    Values for asc1? and asc2? are shown by entering:
      either 'D' (for Dominant) or 'S' (for subordinate).

    Weights must always be entered.

*** BLOCK 2 ***

    For every member a line should be entered containing

    1:   name
    2:   Actualtime   [say, 4.5]
    3:   Totaltime   [say, 8]

where

    name = the name of the member
    Actualtime = the amount of time that that the person actually spends
                   in social interactions
    Totaltime = the total amount of time that the person has available for
                   interactions.

*** BLOCK 3 ***

    For each outside-unit interaction in which a member of the
    unit engages enter line containing

    1:   name
    2:   the activity

where

    name = the member's name
    activity = the name of the activity

*** BLOCK 4 ***

    For every person who was both eligible to join the unit (in
    terms of formal qualifications) and who also wanted to join the unit,
    enter a line containing

    1:   name
    2:   joined?

where

    name = the person's name
    joined? = an indication whether the person joined the unit

    Values for joined? are
        'Y' if the person joined the unit
        'N' if he didn't.

***   BLOCK 5   ***

    For all the unique roles assumed by the overall unit during time T,
    enter a line containing

    1:   role
    2:   roletype

where

    role = the role written exactly as written in the first block of data
    roletype = the type of the role

    Values for roletype can be either 'achieved' or 'ascribed'.
    This is signified by entering
            'ach' for an achieved role
            'asc' for an ascribed role

WARNING !!   Exactly the same spelling must be used for each instance of a
given name. Otherwise, erroneous results occur. For example, let's say that
one person's name in the sample is "John Mc'Doe". Every time that you refer
to him you must enter EXACTLY   "John Mc'Doe"--

            NOT   "John MC'Doe"
            NOR   "John Mc'Doe"
            NOR   "john Mc'Doe"

As far as the computer is concerned, each of the above variants refers to
a completely different person. It will therefore assign your information,
not to YOUR "John Mc'Doe", but to four differnet individuals.
The same warning, of course, applies to role and interaction spelling .

            ***   END OF DETAILS ON DATA INPUT   ***

            ***   SAMPLE INPUT FILE WITH EXECUTION   ***

                          >>>   FILE   <<<
--------------------------------   --------------------------------
Mary Person1,   Duke Person2
role1,   D,   role2,   D,   1,   1
Duke Person2,   John Person5
role3,   D,   role4,   S,   1,   1
Duke Person2,   Jane Person4
role3,   D,   role4,   S,   1,   1
John Person5,   Jane Person4
role5,   D,   role5,   S,   1,   1
Joe Person3,   Jane Person4
role6,   D,   role4,   S,   1,   1

```
Joe Person3,               John Person5
role6,          D,         role4,          S,          1,          1
END,                       END,
END,            END,       END,            END,        1,          1
Duke Person2,   3,         1.5
John Person5,   6,         4
Jane Person4,   5.5,       3.8
Mary Person1,   2,         .5
Joe Person3,    4,         2.5
END,            0,         0
Duke Person2,   Outside-Activity1
Duke Person2,   Outside-Activity2
John Person5,   Outside-Activity3
Jane Person4,   Outside-Activity4
Mary Person1,   Outside-Activity5
Joe Person3,    Outside-Activity6
Joe Person3,    Outside-Activity7
END,            END
John Person5,   Y
Bill Person6,   N
Louise Person7, N
END,            END
role2,    asc
role1,    asc
role3,    ach
role5,    ach
role4,    ach
role6,    ach
END,      END
```

>>>   END-OF-FILE   <<<

-----------------------------------   ---------------------------------

>>>   SAMPLE EXECUTION   <<<

-----------------------------------   ---------------------------------

The interaction-activities represented in the graph:

```
[Mary Person1 / Duke Person2] <role1 <=> role2> [1|1]
[Duke Person2 / John Person5] <role3 <=> role4> [1|1]
[Duke Person2 / Jane Person4] <role3 <=> role4> [1|1]
[John Person5 / Jane Person4] <role5 <=> role5> [1|1]
[Joe Person3 / Jane Person4] <role6 <=> role4> [1|1]
[Joe Person3 / John Person5] <role6 <=> role4> [1|1]
```

```
 # of people modeled in the graph is:  5
Label  1  represents person:  Mary Person1
Label  2  represents person:  Duke Person2
Label  3  represents person:  John Person5
Label  4  represents person:  Jane Person4
Label  5  represents person:  Joe Person3
```

Group Predicates:

PROXIMITY PREDICATE: 0.6942857
----
trans # 1 = 0
trans # 2 = 0.2

```
trans #  3  =  0.5
trans #  4  =  0.5
trans #  5  =  0.3333333
```

TRANSITIVITY PREDICATE: 0.3066667

```
freq  1  =  0.25
freq  2  =  0.5
freq  3  =  0.6666667
freq  4  =  0.6909091
freq  5  =  0.625
```

 FREQUENCY PREDICATE: 0.5465152

```
scope  1  =  0.5
scope  2  =  0.6
scope  3  =  0.75
scope  4  =  0.75
scope  5  =  0.5
```

SCOPE PREDICATE: 0.62

IMPERMEABILITY PREDICATE: 0.6666667

```
Grid Predicates:
Spec  1  =  0.8333333
Spec  2  =  0.6666667
Spec  3  =  0.6666667
Spec  4  =  0.6666667
Spec  5  =  0.8333333
```

SPECIALIZATION PREDICATE: 0.7333333

```
asym  1  =  1
asym  2  =  1
asym  3  =  0.6666667
asym  4  =  0.6666667
asym  5  =  1
```

ASYMMETRY PREDICATE: 0.8666667

```
entitle  1  = 1
entitle  2  = 0.5
entitle  3  = 0
entitle  4  = 0
entitle  5  = 0
```

ENTITLEMENT PREDICATE: 0.3

```
accountability  1  =  0
accountability  2  =  0.6666667
accountability  3  =  1
accountability  4  =  1
accountability  5  =  1
```

ACCOUNTABILITY PREDICATE: 0.7333333

```
-------------------------------------
adjcency matrix:
   0  1  2  3  4  5
1  0  1  0  0  0
2  1  0  1  1  0
3  0  1  0  1  1
4  0  1  1  0  1
5  0  0  1  1  0

set of adjacencies:
   0  1  2  3  4  5
1  0  1  0  0  0
2  1  0  1  1  0
3  0  1  0  1  1
4  0  1  1  0  1
5  0  0  1  1  0

A-P SP  Matrix
   0  1  2  3  4  5
1  0  1  2  2  3
2  1  0  1  1  2
3  2  1  0  1  1
4  2  1  1  0  1
5  3  2  1  1  0
```

STOP at line 00750 of **MAIN PROGRAM**

CAUTION !!!:
        Before you run your own grid-group experiment, you ought to spend some
time learning exactly how to prepare an input file, and how to use the program.
Make up some data, create an input file from them, and run the program. Check
to see whether the scores in the program output agree with the ones that you
have calculated by hand. Then make absolutely sure that all the members of the
on-site experiment team know how to record data in suitable form for this kind
of computer analysis.

Bibliography

Agar, Michael. 1980. *The Professional Stranger: An informal Introduction to Ethnography*. New York: Academic Press.

Atkin, R. H. 1974. *Mathematical Structure in Human Affairs*. New York: Crane & Russak.

Barnes, John. 1979. "Network Analysis: Orientating Nation, Rigorous Technique, or Substantive Field of Study." In Holland and Leinhardt, eds., *Perspectives on Social Network Research*. New York: Academic Press.

Bell, Daniel. 1973. *The Coming of Post-Industrial Society: A Venture in Social Forecasting*. New York: Basic Books.

Bell, Daniel. 1980. *The Winding Passage: Essays and Sociological Journeys 1960–1980*. Cambridge, Mass.: Abt Books.

Benedict, Ruth. 1934. *Patterns of Culture*. Boston: Houghton-Mifflin.

Bernstein, Basil. 1971. "On the Classification and Framing of Educational Knowledge." In B. Bernstein, ed. *Class, Codes, and Control*. Vol. 1. London: Routledge and Kegan Paul.

Boorman, Scott A. and Harrison C. White. 1976. "Social Structures and Multiple Networks II: Role Structures." *American Journal of Sociology* 81:1384–1446.

Campbell, Keith. 1965. "Family Resemblance Predicates. *American Philosophical Quarterly* 2:238–244.

Cunnison, Ian. 1951. *History of the Luapula: An Essay on the Historical Notions of a Central African Tribe*. Rhodes-Livingston Papers 21. Capetown: Oxford University Press.

Cunnison, Ian. 1957. "Histories and Genealogies in a Conquest State." *American Anthropologist* 59:30–31.

Cyert, Richard and James March. 1962. *A Behavioral Theory of the Firm*. Englewood Cliffs, N.J.: Prentice-Hall.

DeFinetti, B. 1974. "The True Subjective Probability Problem."

In C.A.S. Stael von Holstein, ed., *The Concept of Probability in Psychological Experiments*. Dordrecht: Reidel.

Douglas, M. 1970. *Natural Symbols*. London: Barrie and Rockliffe.

Douglas, M. 1978. *Cultural Bias*. Royal Anthropological Institute Occasional Paper No. 35. London.

Douglas, M. 1980. *Edward Evans-Pritchard*. New York: Penguin Press.

Douglas, M., ed. 1982. *Essays in the Sociology of Perception*. London: Routledge and Kegan Paul; New York: Basic Books.

Douglas, M. and J. L. Gross. 1981. "Food and Culture: Measuring the Intricacy of Rule Systems." *Social Science Information* 20:1–35.

Douglas, M. and A. Wildarsky. 1982. *Risk and Culture: An Essay on the Selection of Technical and Environmental Danger*. Berkeley: University of California Press.

Durkheim, E. 1893. *De la Division du Travail Social*. Translated 1933 as *Division of Labor in Society*. New York: Free Press.

Durkheim, E. 1897. *Le Suicide,* tr. 1951 as *Suicide*. New York: Free Press.

Engels, Friedrich. 1886. *Anti-Duhring: Herr Eugen Duhring's Revolution in Science*. Emile Burns, tr. New York: International Publishers, 1936.

Evans-Pritchard, E. E. 1940. *The Nuer*. Oxford: Oxford University Press.

Frank, Ove. 1979. "Sampling and Estimation in Large Social Networks." *Social Networks* 1:91–101.

Freeman, Linton C. 1979. "Centrality in Social Networks: I. Conceptual Clarification." *Social Networks* 1:215–239.

Freeman, Linton C., Douglas Roeder, and Robert Mulholland. 1980. "Centrality in Social Networks: II.Experimental Results." *Social Networks* 2:119–141.

Fried, Morton. 1967. *The Evolution of Political Society*. New York: Random House.

Friedman, J. 1975. "Tribes, States, and Transformations." In M. Bloch, ed., *Marxist Analyses and Social Anthropology*. ASA Studies 2. London: Malaby Press.

Geertz, C. 1973. *The Interpretation of Cultures*. New York: Basic Books.

Granovetter, M. 1979. "The Theory Gap in Social Networks." In Holland and Leinhardt, eds., *Perspectives on Social Network Research*. New York: Academic Press.

Gross, J. L. 1983. "Information-Theoretic Scales for Cultural Rule Systems." In S. Leinhardt, ed., *Sociological Methodology*. San Francisco: Jossey-Bass.

Gross, J. L. 1982. "Measurement of Calendrical Information in Food-Taking Behavior." In M. Douglas, ed., *Food and Culture*. New York: Russell Sage Foundation.

Hampton, James. 1979. "Polymorphous Concepts in Semantic Memory." *Journal of Verbal Learning and Verbal Behavior* 18:441–461.

Hampton, James. 1982. "Giving the Grid/Group Dimensions an Operational Definition." In M. Douglas, ed., *Essays in the Sociology of Perception*. London: Routledge and Kegan Paul.

Harary, F. 1969. *Graph Theory*. Reading, Mass.: Addison-Wesley.

Harary, F., R. Z. Norman, and D. Cartwright. 1965. *Structural Models: An Introduction to the Theory of Directed Graphs*. New York: Wiley.

Holland, P. W. and S. Leinhardt, eds. 1979. *Perspectives on Social Network Research*. New York: Academic Press.

Jeffries, V. and M. E. Ransford. 1980. *Social Stratification: A Multiple Hierarchy Approach*. Boston: Allyn and Bacon.

Johnsrud, Judith. 1977. "A Political Geography of the Nuclear Power Controversy: The Peaceful Atom in Pennsylvania." Ph.D. dissertation, Pennsylvania State University.

Kaprow, Miriam Lee. 1978. "Divided We Stand: A Study of Discord Among Gypsies in a Spanish City." Ph.D. dissertation, Columbia University.

Leach, E. R. 1954. *Political Systems of Highland Burma*. London: G. Bell.

Leinhardt, S. 1976. *Social Networks: A Developing Paradigm*. New York: Academic Press.

Lévi-Strauss, C. 1963. *Structural Anthropology*. New York: Basic Books.

Logan, R. and D. Nelkin. 1980. "Labor and Nuclear Power." *Environment*, 22:6–34.

McLeod, Katrina. 1982. "The Political Culture of Warring States

China." In M. Douglas, ed., *Essays in the Sociology of Perception*. London: Routledge and Kegan Paul.

Maine, Sir Henry James Sumner. 1861. 1963. *Ancient Law: Its Connection with the Early History of Society and Its Relation to Modern Ideas*. Boston: Beacon Press.

March, James and Herbert Simon. 1958. *Organizations*. New York: Wiley.

Marriott, McKim. 1976. "Hindu Transactions: Diversity Without Dualism." In B. Kapferer, ed., *Transactions and Meaning*. Philadelphia: Institute for the Study of Human Issues.

Mars, G. 1982. *Cheats at Work: An Anthology of Workplace Crime*. London: Allen and Unwin.

Needham, Rodney. 1975. "Polythetic Classification." *MAN* (new series), 10:349–369.

Nelkin, D. and M. Pollack. 1980. *The Atom Besieged: Extraparliamentary Dissent in France and Germany*. Cambridge, Mass.: MIT Press.

Ostrander, David. 1982. "One-and Two-Dimensional Models of the Distribution of Beliefs." In M. Douglas, ed., *Essays in the Sociology of Perception*. London: Routledge and Kegan Paul.

Radcliffe-Brown, A. R. 1952. *Structure and Function in Primitive Society*. Glencoe, Ill: Free Press.

Rayner, Steve. 1979. "The Classification and Dynamics of Sectarian Organizations: Grid/Group Perspectives on the Far-Left in Britain." Ph.D. dissertation, University of London.

Rayner, Steve. 1982. "The Perceptions of Time and Space in Egalitarian Sects: A Millenarian Cosmology." In M. Douglas, ed.; *Essays in the Sociology of Perception*. London: Routledge and Kegan Paul.

Roberts, Fred. 1976. *Discrete Mathematical Models*. Englewood Cliffs, N.J.: Prentice-Hall.

Roberts, Fred. 1979. *Measurement Theory: With Applications to Decision-making, Utility, and the Social Sciences*, Reading, Mass.: Addison-Wesley.

Ryle, Gilbert. 1949. *The Concept of Mind*. London: Hutchinson.

Ryle, Gilbert. 1951. "Thinking and Language, III." *Proceedings of the Aristotelian Society* (supplementary series), 25:65–82.

Sahlins, M. D. 1963. "Poor Man, Rich Man, Bigman, Chief:

Political Types in Melanesia and Polynesia." *Comparative Studies in History and Society* 5:285–303.

Schwing, R. and W. Albers, eds. 1980. *Societal Risk Assessment.* New York: Plenum.

Seidman, Stephen. 1981. "Structures Induced by Collections of Subsets: A Hypergraph Approach." *Mathematical Social Sciences* 1:381–396.

Seidman, Stephen B. and Brian L. Foster. 1978. "A Note on the Potential for Genuine Cross-Fertilization Between Anthropology and Mathematics." *Social Networks* 1:65–72.

Seidman, Stephen and Brian L. Foster. 1980. "SONET-1: Social Network Analysis and Modeling System." *Social Networks* 2:85–90.

Self, Peter. 1975. *The Econocrats and the Policy Process: The Politics and Philosophy of Cost-Benefit Analysis.* London: Macmillan; Boulder, Colo.: Westview Press, 1977.

Sorensen, J., J. Soderstrom, R. Bolin, E. Copenhaver, and S. Carnes. 1983. *Restarting TMI Unit One: Social and Psychological Impacts.* Oak Ridge National Laboratory Report ORNL–5891, Oak Ridge, Tenn.

Strathern, Andrew. 1971. *The Rope of Moka: Big-men and Ceremonial Exchange in Mount Hagen, New Guinea.* Cambridge: Cambridge University Press.

Swanson, Guy. 1969. *Rules of Descent: Studies in the Sociology of Parentage.* Ann Arbor: University of Michigan Press.

Thompson, Michael. 1980a. "The Aesthetics of Risk: Culture or Context?" In R. Schwing and W. Albers, eds., *Societal Risk Assessment.* New York: Plenum.

Thompson, Michael. 1980b. "Fission and Fusion in Nuclear Society." RAIN No. 41.

Thompson, Michael. 1981. "Among the Energy Tribes." Working paper of the International Institute for Applied Systems Analysis.

Thompson, Michael. 1982a. "The Problem of the Centre." In M. Douglas, ed., *Essays in the Sociology of Perception.* London: Routledge and Kegan Paul.

Thompson, M. 1982b. "A Three-Dimensional Model." In M. Douglas, ed., *Essays in the Sociology of Perception.* London: Routledge & Kegan Paul.

Vygotsky, L.S. 1962. *Thought and Language*. Kaufman and Vakar, trs. Cambridge, Mass.: MIT Press.

White, H.C., S. A. Boorman, and R. L. Brieger. 1976. "Social Structure from Multiple Networks: I. Blockmodels of Roles and Positions." *American Journal of Sociology* 81:730–780.

Wittgenstein, L. 1953. *Philosophical Notebooks,* Oxford: Blackwell.

Index

Abalone Alliance, 22
Accountability predicate, 70, 92
Accountability score, 81-82; Chamber of Commerce, 102, 109; dunes dwellers, 105, 109; LANE, 107, 109; Local 387, 104, 109; Scallopshell Caucus, 108, 109
Achievement of roles, *see* Roles
Activity/activities, 91, 92, 94, 98-99, 100, 101, 102-3, 104, 105, 107-8; number (i/a), 78; set A, 64, 67, 71, 72
Agar, Michael, 88, 97
Aggregate/composite, grid score, ix, 82-83, 85; Chamber of Commerce, 102, 109; dunes dwellers, 105, 109; LANE, 107, 109; Local 387, 104, 109; Scallopshell Caucus, 108, 109
Aggregate/composite, group score, 82-83, 85; Chamber of Commerce, 101, 109; dunes dwellers, 104, 109; LANE, 106, 109; Local 387, 103, 109; Scallopshell Caucus, 108, 109
Albers, W., 2
Ascription of roles, *see* Roles
Asymmetry predicate, 70
Asymmetry score, 80-81; Chamber of Commerce, 102, 109; dunes dwellers, 105, 109; LANE, 106, 109; Local 387, 103, 109; Scallopshell Caucus, 108, 109
Atkin, R.H., 92
Autonomy, 114

Barnes, John, 67
Basic predicates, 60-62, 66, 82-85; *see also* Accountability predicate; Asymmetry predicate; Entitlement predicate; Frequency predicate; Impermeability predicate; Proximity predicate; Scope predicate; Specialization predicate; Transitivity predicate
Bell, Daniel, 17
Benedict, Ruth, 8, 10, 111
Bernstein, B., 11
Big-men, Highland New Guinea, 8, 14
Bongo-Bongoism, 16, 17
Boorman, S. A., 67
Brieger, R. L., 67
British social workers, 9
Bureaucracy, 9, 48, 52-53, 68

Campbell, Keith, 60
Cashiers, supermarket, 9
Chamber of Commerce (Lakemouth), 22, 25, 28, 29, 31, 35, 49, 65, 67, 68, 93, 94, 95, 96, 97; cultural bias, 52-53; and grid-group assessment, 35, 36, 37-39, 40, 41, 48, 98-102, 103, 104, 109
Chan Kingdom, ancient China, 10
Children of Jupiter, 27, 36, 50
Citizens of Lakemouth: Jack Loveland, 30-31, 36-37, 49, 94, 102; T. R. Prendle, 26-27, 36-37, 49
Civil service, 9
Clamshell Alliance, 22
Coastal Gas and Electric, 24, 25-31, 35, 36, 51
Collectivity, 15
Commitment, to social units, *see* Social unit(s)
Commonality of experience, 79
Comparison, ix, 16, 36, 37, 63, 83-84; and generalization, 16, 19
Competition, 6, 43
Cosmology, x, xiii, 15, 35, 36, 50, 52, 53, 55, 56, 91, 110, 113, 114, 115
Cost/benefit analysis, 2